KV-193-172

Chapman 87
The State of British Poetry

Illustrations by Alfons Bytautas, John MacWilliam, Robin Spark and David Stephenson

ISBN 0 906772 83 4   ISSN 0308-2695   © *Chapman* 1997

CHAPMAN
4 Broughton Place, Edinburgh EH1 3RX, Scotland
E-mail: chapman@compura.com.uk
Tel 0131–557 2207   Fax 0131–556 9565
Editor: Joy Hendry   **Assistant Editor: Gerry Stewart**
Volunteers: Valerie Brotherton, Sarah Bryant, Eva Freischläger, John Edwards, Sarah Edwards, C J Lindsay, Paula Middleton.

Submissions:
Chapman welcomes submissions of poetry, fiction and articles provided they are accompanied by a stamped addressed envelope or International Reply Coupons

Subscriptions:

	Personal		Institutional	
	1 year	2 years	1 year	2 years
UK	£15	£28	£20	£37
Overseas	£20/$34	£37/$62	£25/$42	£45/$74

THE SCOTTISH ARTS COUNCIL

•EDINBVRGH•
THE CITY OF EDINBURGH COUNCIL

Printed by The Cromwell Press Ltd., Brougton Gifford, Melksham, Wiltshire SN12 8PH

Editorial

British and Irish Poetry in the Making: University of Salzburg, November, 1996

Why should the University of Salzburg host a conference on British and Irish Poetry in the Making? Why not? But there's a deeper answer: a certain James Hogg. Not the Ettrick Shepherd, but a recently retired and visionary professor at Salzburg's Institut Für Anglistik und Amerikanistik. He claims no descent from our James Hogg, but suspects antecedents in the Borders, and perhaps these genes stimulated him to spend the last thirty years developing his individual view of British poetry, and actively promoting it.

Hogg's inspiration stems from his refusal to slavishly follow international poetic fashion. He became conscious that there were unpopular factions in British poetry, including becoming intensely aware of the individuality and quality of Scottish poetry long before it had aroused much world interest. He realised that there were remarkable poets and academics, like Tom Scott, Peter Russell, William Oxley and Fred Beake, like Professor Anthony L. Johnson of the University of Pisa, who weren't getting the oxygen of publicity, or sometimes even proper publication. This has resulted in a steady stream of publications from the University of Salzburg Press of the work of these writers – and this particular conference.

One remarkable aspect of Hogg's influence has been his emphasis on the importance to literary and creative life of so-called 'Little Magazines', magazines like *Chapman, The Honest Ulsterman, Acumen* and *Iron*. This awareness has led to the publication of a huge tome on British Literary Magazines, the size of the London telephone directory, written by Wolfgang Görtschacher, organiser of this conference, something never published in Britain, nor ever likely to be. The role of these and other 'little magazines' figured prominently in the conference programme.

That's the background, one which might provoke us to review our own poetic assumptions. So the conference brought together some of these people to discuss the making of British poetry. Having entitled my paper, pretentiously: 'How Poems Make the People', I opened the conference, my thesis- an account of how poetry has played an important role in the development of Scottish cultural awareness over this century, importantly influencing both political and social trends, and how we see the poet as part of a community, not an elitist exile, necessarily divorced from society. This dichotomy turned out to be a preoccupation of the conference, the Scottish viewpoint amplified by other Scots, Anne MacLeod and Angus Dunn, and by others like Peter Mortimer, editor of *Iron*, and Tom Clyde of *The Honest Ulsterman*. There was something of a north-south divide, the north of England, Scotland and Ireland versus the south of England. There was also a noticeable divide between, if you like, the 'practitioners' at the conference, that is, the poets and editors and the academics.

One controversial contribution came from Jon Corelis, an ex-academic and poet from Silicon Valley in the States, who had been invited to sum up British poetry from the perspective of blissful ignorance and had set to work trawling the anthologies and magazines with a will. His analysis pleased some and displeased others greatly, which was his intention, of course, and clearly he thoroughly enjoyed doing it, although it was done gently and with wit. Thinking his contribution to be so thought-provoking and interesting, I asked him to expand it as the key-note article in this issue. Briefly, he divides British poetry into five broad schools:

1. the Scottish school including some non-Scots doing similar things:

2. the Suburban School "excessively quotidian" but well-written, poetry exemplified by the phrase – "Darling, here's what happened":

3. the Urbanites, or City Kids, hip neo-surrealists keen to get their work on the Internet:

4. the Academics, crafted, learned stuff such as written by Peter Porter:

5. the Starters Over – the eclectics –people looking for a new beginning but probably not finding it.

I summarise his findings here briefly, and commend you to his article for further elucidation and amusement.

Since his paper followed mine immediately, I could have hardly set him up to assert his preference for the Scottish school for its warmth, vitality, its "singingness", and he singled out as outstanding poets like Tom Scott, Maureen Sangster and Gerry Cambridge, scarcely household names here. Yes, so much for a different perspective. This theme of a playful analysis of the writers' art and craft, and attitudes towards it is continued in Neil K Henderson's article, 'Loveable Warts: a Defence of Self-Indulgence'. Jon Corelis's paper further inspired me to commission the Mexican writer, Juan Luis Campos, newly returned to Mexico after five years in Scotland, to write a parallel piece on Scottish writing to appear in a future issue.

For me, and I think for everybody, one of the most constructive aspects of the conference was the chance to exchange circumstances, visions, viewpoints and problems with other literary editors outside Scotland. Patricia Oxley of *Acumen* produced a lovely phrase about editors as people "educating themselves in public", via their magazines and Peter Mortimer of *Iron* described a magazine as "a handbook for a revolution". More may come of it, as there was a recent reunion of the British contingent in Salisbury in June, which unfortunately I was unable to attend. But perhaps most eye-opening of all was the realisation that in Austria, among the Salzburg mountains, people were looking at the poetry of these islands from a very different point of view than is promoted here by the media and academic poetic orthodoxy, both north and south of the border.

Finally, and sadly, the death occurred recently of T S Law, prolific poet and tireless advocate of unique Scottish character and culture, and also of Professor Robert Silver, polymath, scientist and poet. Both were truly remarkable men, Bob Silver's scientific achievements are widely known, but typically, and ironically in line with the spirit of the Salzburg conference, and shamefully, much of Tom Law's remains unpublished and his epic achievement is still to be recognised, both at home and abroad.

From Scotland to Suburbia:
A Landscape of Current British Poetry
Jon Corelis

The perceptions of one's own country by a stranger may be puzzling, irritating or amusing, but they are bound, if they are honest, to be educational, since seeing the familiar through an untutored set of eyes can not fail to give one a new perspective on it. This lesson was brought home to me in a small way some years ago, when I made the acquaintance of a young Greek who had come to pursue postgraduate studies at a university in California. After I got to know him a bit, he asked one day if he could put a question to me. Why, he wondered, were there so many insane people in the United States? I replied that I wasn't very happy either about what was going on in Washington. But it turned out that his question was not a figure of speech: he wanted to know why so many people who clearly had mental health problems were to be seen wandering the streets of America's cities.

I remembered my Greek friend's question later when I was introduced to a Japanese engineer who had just arrived in the US. What, I asked him, was the most surprising thing he found in America? The huge size of people's living quarters, he answered immediately, and to me, surprisingly, since I happened to know that the apartments in the building where he was living were by American standards tiny.

On reflection, I found these perceptions not only startling, but also educational. I knew of course that Japanese homes tended to be small, and that Greece's social welfare programmes and strongly family-based society provided almost everyone with at least enough care to keep them off the street. But it would never have occurred to me that these particular manifestations of American affluence and of American social dysfunction had progressed to the point where they would be the first things which a foreigner would notice.

It is in the hope that my own callow observations on the contemporary British poetry scene may similarly because of their very naiveté prove of interest that I have undertaken to set them forth here in the following survey of the current British poetry scene by one who is an outsider to it. The purpose of my remarks is not to pass any definitive judgements on the state of that scene, a task for which I am hardly qualified, but rather to provoke the sort of puzzlement, irritation or amusement (and if at my own expense, so be it) which might initiate in my readers a train of thought which can lead them to a new perspective on their own poetic world.

Not, however, that I have no qualifications for the task beyond my own lack of preconceptions. Though my own reputation as a poet is tiny, it is there, and is based primarily on the generosity with which a handful of British poets and editors have received my work. Moreover, British poetry from Chaucer to Dylan Thomas has been a life-long love and study of mine. But my familiarity with more recent British poetry has heretofore been confined to a limited acquaintance with a few of the most prominent names. Nor may I justly claim to provide any insight on the subject as an American poet or an American critic, since such a claim would imply a substantial involvement with the contemporary poetry scene in America, whereas my own modest poetic work has been accomplished in almost complete isolation from the current literary and academic establishments of my own country. A further difficulty was imposed by another sort of isolation: living as I do six thousand miles from London, the sources of very current British verse available to me are scarce and erratic.

I have nevertheless been able to put together what I hope is a roughly accurate map of much of the state of British poetry over the last three to four years, based on the poetic content of recent issues of such magazines as *Acumen, Agenda, Ambit, Angel Exhaust, Chapman, The Dark Horse, London Magazine, The London Review of Books, Madam X, The Poet's Voice, Poetry London Newsletter, Poetry Review, PN Review, Rialto, Stand, Swansea Review, Tabla* and *The Times Literary Supplement*, collections by current British poets, mostly published since 1994, from Bloodaxe, Carcanet, Peterloo, Smith/Doorstop and The University of Salzburg Press, the majority of the Oxford Poets volumes published in that same period, and a few other sources. I also was able to gather quite a bit of material from the Internet, in forms which I will describe later. That this material despite its diversity represents a rather random sampling of the current poetic scene in Britain may be as much an advantage as the reverse: if it means that I have missed important areas of activity and overemphasized peripheral ones, it also ensures that no preconceptions will have been smuggled into my interpretations due to their being based on material selected according to pre-existing notions of its proper significance.

There has emerged in my mind from my experience of this literature a landscape of current British poetry as including five schools of poets, who practice five types of styles. These schools are not very sharply defined: most poets only more or less belong to one, and some poets can be put into more than one. The styles also are to be considered more as general tendencies than as absolutely definable genres; and though I find that each style tends to be particularly characteristic of one group, in practice you can find examples of most of the styles in most of the groups. In spite of their blurred boundaries, I feel that the schools and styles are identifiable enough for it to make sense to talk about them.

The first clear impression I formed when I began my research was that today's best British poetry, or at least that which is most to my taste, is associated with Scotland – I mean by this the work of poets who publish in Scottish magazines, or whom I have found in other magazines but whom I infer from various indications to have a Scottish background (and it might be appropriate to add here that the present essay was researched and to a very great extent written before I had any idea that it might eventually be published in a Scottish magazine). These poets constitute the first of the schools I have perceived, and I will for convenience call them the Scottish school, even though some of its members may not actually be from or in Scotland.

The work of these Scottish poets exemplifies many of the qualities which I personally find most appealing in poetry: a diction which is both naturally colloquial and deliberately poetic, the ability to express intense emotion with unapologetic directness but without sentimentality, an unaffected delight in lyric songfulness, an ability to be humorous while still being serious and, often, a non-polemical political and social consciousness which gains conviction from the quietness of its rage. These are, I think, old fashioned virtues, or at least currently neglected ones. At any rate, Scottish poetry seems to me to have kept alive the great modernist tradition which started to fall into discredit in Britain and America around 1950. Indeed, to read today's Scottish poets, one might think that the great post-modernist revolution in British and American poetry had never happened. Nor is this their only attractive quality. Although other poets, such as John Lyons and Matt Simpson, have made interesting attempts to make dialectical English of various sorts into a credible vehicle for modern verse, it is the Scottish school which by far makes the most extensive and ambitious attempts to employ the resources of dialect for other than strictly comic ends. For example, of all the poems which I read in preparation for these remarks, I thought that one of the most purely wonderful was W S Milne's translation of a lengthy passage from Dante into the thickest of Lallans. Another appealing feature of many Scottish poets is their ability to write verse with political implications which gains in credibility by its lack of ideological tendentiousness. For example, the work of a number of Scottish women poets, such as Maureen Sangster and Joan Lennon, seems to me to illustrate how effective feminist poetry can be when it eschews any externally determined political agenda and instead gains its authority by speaking honestly from a position which could be imaginatively realized only by a female consciousness.

I further find the Scottish poets to be the most distinguished practitioners of two of the stylistic trends which I have perceived in current British verse. The first of these is the Lyric style, by which I mean pretty much the text-book definition: a short, melodic poem expressing erotic, melancholy or exuberant emotion. Lyric of course is commonly found also among other schools, but elsewhere it usually seems very much an exercise; by and large, it is only the Scottish poets who seem to have kept the ability to write lyrics which are emotional expressions rather than literary demonstrations. For instance, it almost only among them that I have found lyrics which I could imagine someone in real life actually giving to someone else whom they wanted to seduce. More generally, the songfulness of Scottish poetry even in non-lyric modes is something I too often miss elsewhere. Even a random glance through the poets I've mentioned reveals an instinctive songfulness as a common element among radically different styles, from the Neolithic chant of George Mackay Brown:

> Who's at the Hoy shore, by starlight
> Simmering two fish?
> The King of Stars and Oceans.

to the balladic reel of W N Herbert:

> Noo gaither roond baith quine and loon
> and a nitherin screed Eh'll read
> o hoo auld Scrapie Powrie stole

thi sowels of thi still-waurm deid.

the pure folk song of R L Cook:

> Come awa in ben
> Come oot o' the stour,
> Dark is the nicht
> Oot there, an dour.

the Dylan Thomas-like oracular tolling of Sam Gilliland:

> Where long dead sorrows melted in my mouth,
> And cherry nipples arched to a dappled sun
> That fledged the marrow of my youth

the dialectical resonance of Gerry Cambridge:

> Oa, cum an in an doan't stand at thee doar!
> I doan't get meny cum ti see me noo.

the slyly precise aural interweavings of Anne MacLeod:

> My scales slip so sweetly,
> my tongue forks so
> neatly. I
> swallow
>   completely.

and even in a less traditionally lyric poet such as Robin Bell, who can evoke a music which suggests an atonal Wallace Stevens:

> I try to picture you
> in that east-facing room,
> the sky a hot blue,
> waves of pear blossom
> at the tall window.

Whatever their stylistic differences, none of these poets has forgotten that poetry is utterance, not scribbling. It is significant that Tom Scott, one of the finest of Scottish poets and perhaps the most impressively songful of all, indicated that he considered the art of sound to be the salient characteristic which raises poetry above the level of being mere verse in his comment, "Poetry is verse that sings with its own unique music."

The second style which I find particularly characteristic of the Scottish school, though again it is not their exclusive property, is what I would call the Colloquialist. Colloquialist poems are written in language which is deliberately vernacular, everyday and non-academic. In the hands of a skilled poet, it can be at the same time quite poetic. Many Colloquialist poems are dramatic monologues giving a 'slice of life' episode that sums up an important aspect of the speaker's existence, often in a manner reminiscent of Browning. Sometimes these dramatic monologues, like Browning's, are historical set-pieces; others employ a contemporary setting in order to make a political or social statement rather than a historical one. In such monologues – recent examples include Jackie Kay's 'Ghost of a Girl Collier, 1837' and Gerry Cambridge's 'An Old Crofter Speaks' – we see brilliant realisations of one of the most important points in the modernist agenda, the revelation of the genuinely tragic stature of very ordinary lives.

Other Colloquialist poems – good examples would be some other of the poems of the versatile Jackie Kay – are less formal and less traditionally literary monologues, characterised by contemporary themes, a lively, often comic, diction and vivid, sometimes racy playing with everyday language, along with an underlying seriousness. In this combination of qualities, this particular variant of the Colloquialist style might be compared with the best of the stand-up comic genre – I'm thinking of people such as Lord Buckley, Lennie Bruce, Richard Pryor or George Carlin, who are verbal artists on a level that the faintly derogatory term stand-up comic fails to convey. Though poems in the Colloquialist style sometimes risk the danger of descending into the banality of mere entertainment, I think that at its best verse in this style is one of the most admirable things happening in the current British poetry scene, since it provides an example of a valid poetic which is particularly well and effectively integrated within its general culture.

It occurs to me that I might clarify the appeal of today's Scottish poetry by invoking a concept which could also prove useful later in describing my reaction to other schools. That concept I call the implicit preface. I believe that any poem can be seen as having a preface which derives from the culture in which it is written. Occasionally this preface is made explicit, as with the ancient Greeks in the most famous of all such prefaces, "Sing, goddess". But more often the preface is left implicit: for the Imperial Romans, for instance, that preface was, "Here is a poem worthy of what our culture must now be"; for medieval poets it was, "Here is a prayer", for the Elizabethans, "This is our new world". Victorian poets, with their magisterial sense of moral obligation, might be said to preface their works, "It is my duty to inform you...", while the poetry of the first half of the twentieth century, which is what I mean by the modernist era, begins "Here is a way to make sense of this mess". The Scottish poets, with their instinctive songfulness and unassuming though impressive technical skill and clear sense of commonality with their wider society, seem to me to preface their poems, "Here is a song I wrote".

The poets of the second school which emerged from my experience of current British verse are associated with a geography, not of the map, but of the mind. Their poems seem to take place in a generic, somewhat posh, suburban landscape which could be anywhere: neat, prosperous houses, manicured gardens, terribly nice people. This is the home ground of this second school, and the setting for most of their work. I will therefore call them the Suburbanites. The phrase may be a bit misleading, since their poetic environment is not confined strictly to suburbia, but even when their poems are explicitly set in a city, it seems to be in one of the leafier, gentrified, low-density neighbourhoods rather than in the gritty urban core. But more often, the identification with bedroom communities is quite open: one poet whom I associate with this school has even written a sequence of poems entitled "Suburban Myths".

It would be difficult to imagine a group more different from the Scots. Indeed, when I progressed from the Scottish poets to the Suburbanite ones, I felt as if I had wandered out of a conclave of bards and stumbled upon a creative writing workshop. Suburbanite verse tends to be aggressively quotidian in its content, which is typically marked by familiar references to driving the family car, watching TV, putting the kids to bed, divorcing and taking a lover, looking at old snapshots and remembering one's grandmother. This poetry seems to be aimed at a comfortable, upper-middle-class suburban audience, to whom it offers the same sort of pleasure of recognition as do the "lifestyle" articles one finds in the feature section of the newspapers, on topics such as "Problems with a Step-daughter," or "Encountering an Ex-Lover" or "Are We Numb to Violence on the News?" One, at least if one is a certain kind of a one, reads these things with narcissistic delight: why, that's just what my friends and I talk about. All in all, I would say that the implicit preface of this school's poems is, "Darling, guess what's happened!"

The Suburbanites, if I understand them (which I admit I may not), conceive poetry as a vehicle for transforming muted personal anxieties into thoughtful exercises in literary craftsmanship, and I have come to think of their way of writing as the Well-Crafted style. Much of this sort of poetry follows the same, predictable rhetorical strategy. It begins with a teaser, a rhetorical tugging at your sleeve to get you interested in what's about to happen. Many of these teasers aim at arousing a puzzled interest by employing the Pronoun Mysterious in the first line: "Driving to meet you...", or "She had always hated orange". Alternatively it can present an unexplained portrait, on the assumption that we'll respond by wanting it explained: "Roses litter the frosty alley...", or "The women are singing in the patisserie". And there are other techniques. Then comes the pitch, the substance of the poem as a satisfaction of the sense of incompleteness which the teaser has deliberately aroused. And finally, in the last line or two, the fillip: a brief, striking, pithy sentence or phrase which uses wit, irony, or humour to reinforce, undercut or give a new perspective on the pitch: "But chocolate never tasted right again", or "'I knew he'd let us down,' says Sandra". Three of the preceding six examples I have made up in the spirit of parody; the remaining three are actual quotes from Suburbanite poets. It will no doubt be obvious to the reader which are which.

It is clear where this teaser-pitch-fillip pattern comes from: it is the standard rhetorical strategy of advertising. Look at almost any advertisement in any medium and you are likely to find an example. For example, I have before me as I write this a recent issue of *The Economist* magazine, which contains a full page ad for IBM headed, in huge blue letters, CARRIER PIGEONS. This is a teaser aimed at making me say, "Carrier pigeons? What can that have to do with IBM?" Reading the ad's text to satisfy my curiosity, I'm given the pitch that no matter how much communications hardware a world-wide business may have – fax machines, phones, email, even carrier pigeons – it still needs a business database, and IBM specialises in supporting such databases for its customers world wide. The article ends with the highlighted phrase, "IBM: Solutions for a small planet," a fillip which puts a clever slant on the ad's theme of IBM's world-wide database services to suggest with bland effrontery that this huge and ruthless multi-national corporation is a member in good standing of the Greens. It really shouldn't be too surprising that even poets are influenced by this rhetorical strategy, since they like everyone else in our society are exposed to it dozens of times a day.

In addition to a standardised rhetorical structure, the Well-Crafted style is characterised by a predilection for a few particular types of ornamentation. One popular trope is the Brief Catalogue, a series of three or four related words or phrases, such as "walls, clock, kettle", or "eyes, brows and chins", or "chat, chips and baked beans". Apparently the rule is that you may do this once, and only once, per poem. A related and even more common device is the "deep, blue sea" construction, consisting of a sensitively chosen adjective followed by an even more sensitively chosen adjective, after which, to great fanfare, enter the noun: "soft, uneasy huffs", "babbling, silvered sky", "cool, surgical music", "immense, empty prairie," or "dark, impossible bridge". (The foregoing are all real examples.) Another quality which particularly marks this group is that a remarkably high percentage of their poems occupy between two thirds of, and exactly one, page, as if their authors had in mind maximising their output's marketability by providing editors with conveniently page-sized blocks of verse.

Suburbanitism is a tendency rather than an absolute category, and many of its practitioners can be seen as belonging also to other schools; in particular, there is a great deal of similarity and even overlap between the Suburbanites and the Academic school which I shall describe presently. But perhaps the most purely Suburbanite poets whom I have encountered are Julia Copus, Katherine Frost, Carol Satyamurti, and Penelope Shuttle, with Suburbanite influence also perceptible in Maura Dooley and Moniza Alvi, though these latter two succeed in some of their poems in escaping it. It should be pointed out that what unites these authors is a style rather than a subject matter; most of these poets also write poems which are deliberately removed from the Suburban milieu, which nevertheless still exhibit the Well-Crafted style and other Suburbanite characteristics; while on the other hand, the verse of Stewart Conn demonstrates that it is possible to write poems about the home routines of contemporary life without being a Suburbanite in the literary sense, though this may have something to do with his being a Scot.

Well, taste is the king of all, and although the ubiquitousness of this type of poetry is evidence that it is to many people's, I have no doubt been unable to conceal that it is not to mine. I have much more positive though ambiguous feelings about the poets of the next school that emerged from my explorations, whom I call the City Kids, because they are (at least as one conceives them from the imagery and tone of their poems) young, urban and hip. I take them to be the avant garde of the current British verse scene; certainly they are the ones who seem to me most seriously experimental and most committed to extending the resources of language in order to explore fundamentally new ways of saying things. Poems which I have seen by Michael Ayres, David Bircumshaw and Norman Jope are particularly good examples of this school.

The style most closely associated with the City Kids is what I would call neo-surrealist, since it tries to extend the surrealist agenda along the lines pioneered by William Burroughs, whose "cut-up technique" attempts to

Illustration by John MacWilliam

create, not (as the surrealists did) a language which could go beyond ordinary meaning in order to reveal the deep structures of the mind, but rather a language which could go beyond meaning itself. Two lines from a recent poem by Anthony Barnett seem to sum up the neo-surrealist method:

You see, I mix up my words in a
confrontation between vacuum and atmosphere

The neo-surrealist style of the City Kids has, I think, major virtues and major weaknesses. In its attempt to go beyond meaning, neo-surrealism raises inarticulateness to a means of elaborate expression: the unspoken preface to this type of poem might be, "Well, like, man, you know..." The language employed by these poets reminds me of Homer's description of Odysseus, whose flow of words was like a blizzard of rhetoric dazzling his hearers. But whereas Odysseus's verbal blizzard was meant to smother all reluctance to be persuaded, the City Kids in their neo-surrealist verbal blizzards seem interested in covering up the streets and hills and trees of reality with a deep blanket of linguistic snow just for the pleasure of then being able to contemplate the weirdly abstract new contours of the resulting world. These lines from Norman Jope's prose poem 'Cornucopia' are a good illustration of what I mean:

Roads of black olives, trampled; sleepers zebra'd with
an onyx mud slashed over turquoise glebes, desert fringing
them with skins of caramel that marslight varnishes; such
are the lineaments of other kingdoms. Here is a horn of
plaster, melted cheeses sleeking under, the skies condensed
to milkwhite weather fronts.

That is as fascinating as a kaleidoscope; the question is whether it is any more meaningful. At their best, these poets can make us look at language itself differently, which is a considerable contribution, and which makes large patches of their work intriguing on a first reading. But I'm not sure if their method has the potential to do more than that. The risk of literary experimentation is that the new and interesting pathways it opens up may turn out to be dead ends. The City Kids deserve a great deal of respect for taking that risk; in my opinion it remains to be seen whether it will pay off.

It is possible that the City Kids bulk larger in my impression of the current British poetry scene than they would in that of most of my readers because they are the school which has so far best established its presence on the Internet, which made their poems as easily accessible to me in California as any published in San Francisco. I would like to digress and expand briefly on this subject to offer a few speculations on the propagation of British verse. In order to do so, I must first describe the present character of that propagation as I understand it.

As I read through the current British verse available to me, I formed an impression of a rough but clear sort of *cursus honorum* among British poets, consisting of successive publication in 1) student and very local or short-lived poetry magazines, 2) small but well-established regional magazines which one British poet of my acquaintance has described as "hobbyist", 3) the more prominent regionally based magazines which have a national reputation, 4) major national magazines like *Agenda, Chapman* or *London Magazine*, or inclusion in an anthology published by a highly regarded commercial or academic publisher, leading finally to 5) induction into the Valhalla of an individual Selected or Collected poems by such a publisher. No doubt the situation is more complex than this, and I haven't been able to take into account such factors as performance or prize competitions, but at least a couple of the British poets to whom I have communicated this impression have told me that overall it is generally recognisable.

The key concept underlying such a situation is that of a hierarchy of prestige among the various channels for communicating poetry. At the very bottom are methods such as posting one's poems on the sides of buildings or reciting them in pubs in exchange for a pint: though this may be publication in the broad meaning of the term, it is not considered real publication in the careerist sense. Real publications have three characteristics: they are printed on paper bound into books or magazines, they are sold in shops or by subscription, and they are refereed by editors with generally recognised credentials for doing so. It is this last point that chiefly determines the amount of realness – that is, the prestige – of a given publication: the greater the respect commanded by the academic or commercial institutions with which the referees are associated, the more real, or prestigious, the publication will be.

The impact of this way of propagating poetry on the poetic life of a nation is immense, since it has the effect of establishing a structured class of literary mandarins as the arbiters of what type of poetry will be encouraged to establish itself. And because its own prestige depends on the legitimacy of current perceptions of literary and academic respectability, this class, whatever their politics may be, will in the literary sense be deeply conservative.

It is no doubt rash to predict the future course of either literature or technology, but since poets are supposed to be prophets, I will take the risk and predict that the Internet will bring about the end of the predominance of this hierarchy of poetic respectability. It will do so, I believe, by eroding that hierarchy's most fundamental power: the ability to attribute different amounts of realness to various publications. The appearance of on-line magazines with a professional level of design is already making it difficult to define a hierarchy of prestige in verse propagated via the Internet, and fortunately the situation is very likely in the future to become even more confusing. If these trends continue, the effect could be the increasing isolation, and eventually the supplanting, of the currently established hierarchy of verse publication by a much more freewheeling and diverse body of work which will be exempt from the necessity of conforming to the requirements of the literary mandarins and will thus really be free to establish its worth by competition in the marketplace of public taste.

I suspect that the developments which I have just predicted will be particularly unwelcome among the poetic school which I am about to describe now, and which I call the Academics, for two reasons. First, it is apparent from references in their own poetry that they often are academics in the proper sense, that is, faculty members at colleges and universities. But their work is also academic in the wider, descriptive sense of being formal, bookish, and in conformance to an implicitly shared body of rules. In spite of their frequent modernistic acceptance of traditionally unpoetic subject matter, there is something about these poets that recalls the eighteenth century, when the right style was considered to be that practiced by the right people, the right people being those who practiced the right style.

And in fact this Academic school is the one which is most closely of all associated with a single dominant style, which I have therefore come to call the Academic style. It is this style which separates the Academics from their close relations the Suburbanites, with whom they seem to share the same upper middle class milieu and concerns. The Academic style is typically characterised by the display of traditional humanistic learning and a high degree of technical poetic skill. Rhyme, either full or slant, is often used with remarkable deftness, and the flow of imagery is maintained with both vividness and discipline.

Among the poets who share these general stylistic characteristics, a number of subspecies may be distinguished. One of these I would call the Pure Professors, since their work is the most purely Academic stylistically, leaving the most distinct impression of, as Peter Mortimer has written, "the verse of the academic, like the faint hint of a passing perfume". The clearest examples in my experience are probably Peter Porter, Lawrence Sail and Charles Tomlinson, all of whose work is characterised by such consistent elegance, thoughtfulness and craftsmanship that I found I could not get through any one of their collections of verse without starting to groan towards the end, "Oh God, not another one!" Another group might be called Safe Experimentalists, since they, like the City Kids, are engaged in what is ostensibly experimental poetry, but unlike those impressionistic anarchists, they avoid the risks involved in experimentation by confining themselves to carefully controlled repetitions of experiments which have long since proved profitable – for instance, George Szirtes's use of such innovative techniques as drawing parallels between poetry and photography or refurbishing the symbols of classical literature as a context for treating important contemporary problems like the turmoil in Eastern Europe, or Christopher Middleton's bold explorations of territory minutely mapped by Wallace Stevens over half a century ago. A third subset, or perhaps it should be called a small related school, is Academic in that its primary goal seems to be to demonstrate that you can too write good and accessible poems about contemporary life. This group I find the most readable of the Academics. An example is Ron Butlin, whose poetry, if it too often reads like examples provided by a creative writing workshop leader, is still enjoyable and unpretentious. Perhaps here as in the case of Stewart Conn we have the case of a poet whom the salubrious influence of Scotland has enabled to rise above his category.

In addition to its manifest skill, the Academic style is marked also by a reluctance directly to express intense emotion, which seems to me a very strange characteristic for a poetry to have. I read the Academics with admiration, but I am always left wondering what all this ingenuity is in service of: I put down their poems with a feeling of impressive technique in search of something to mean, and a reluctant conclusion that the technique of the Academics is exercised ultimately for its own sake. Accordingly I must report if I am to be honest that, as impressed as I am by the undeniable accomplishments of these poets, emotionally most of their work leaves me cold.

I think that the reason for this failure to mean in emotional terms derives, paradoxically, exactly from the fact of the Academic school's success. The Academic poet's primary goal, I suspect, is to establish and retain membership in a currently dominant school of poetry by demonstrating that he or she is able to employ the right style and therefore must be one of the right people. The implicit preface of this type of poetry is, "Here are my credentials". Those credentials compel respect for their skill and learning. But they do not for me fill the emotional hole at the heart of this type of poetry.

This credentialing process, that is, this claim to official relevance and credibility, can also be seen at work, I think, in the nature of the titles which currently tend to be given to the collections of poetry published by the most well established presses. Like the names of business firms, the titles of these books are carefully constructed to convey a definite image, if possible an image which will suggest by flattery that the business (or poetry) in question has a claim to the attention of, and a proper place in the life of, the potential customer (or reader). In the commercial sphere, a good example of what I mean is the name of a wildly popular restaurant chain, Hard Rock Cafe, which suggests to its patrons an alluring combination of retro innocence and bohemian sophistication. For examples from the literary world, consider the titles of a random selection of poetry books, the majority of them authored by Academics or their close relations the Suburbanites, published by prestigious presses in the past few years: *Best China Sky, Blind Field, Bridge Passages, Building a City for Jamie, Building into Air, Changing the Subject, Histories of Desire, Intimate Chronicles, Jubilation, Maiden Speech, Millennial Fables, News from the Front, Phrase Book, Possible Worlds, Provisions of Light, Striking Distance, Taxing the Rain, The Air Show, The Chair of Babel, The Country at my Shoulder, The Door in the Wall, The Shuttered Eye.* The first thing one notices about these titles is the prevalence of puns. "Bridge Passages", for instance, can be segments of music or pieces of writing about real or metaphorical bridges; "Changing the Subject" can mean switching to another topic or altering the consciousness of a perceiver; and similar word plays may be seen in most of the other titles. This use of puns is intended to create an image of the author as someone who is playfully yet seriously creative with language, and also to rope us into reading the book by giving us at the outset the pleasure of a small joke which we are intelligent enough to share with the author. On further examination, a second quality of many of these titles becomes clear: they offer us a promise, as attractive as it is absurd, that poetry will enable us to overcome the impotence to participate meaningfully in society and in history which has been imposed on us by current political and cultural conditions. "Building a City for Jamie", for instance, or "Intimate Chronicles", or "Histories of Desire", all suggest that we can derive from various types of personal relationships, and from the poetry written about them, a sense of significance equal to that which we could gain from meaningfully affecting the historical process, if it were possible for us to do such a thing.

The final school which I perceive in current British poetry is not really a school, but an eclectic collection of poets who don't at all belong to any of the other schools. For a long time I could not think of a name to put to them, but it finally dawned on me that they all did seem to have one thing in common: they have to a significant extent rejected the post-modernist traditions which have dominated English-language poetry since the mid-century. I will call them the Starters-Over, because I see in them an attempt to return to the great Anglo-American modernist tradition of Yeats, Pound, Eliot, Stevens, William Carlos Williams and Dylan Thomas, not in order to imitate or revive it (since we cannot follow an antique drum), but to use it as a place to back up to, a place from which to start over again in hope of finding new directions in poetry which will be more valid than the post-modernist trends which also started from there. I imagine their poems as being prefaced, "Here is how we should be doing it, maybe".

I would include in this class James Keery, a master of quiet technique whose nature poems achieve a Japanese minuteness of observation; John Lyons, who uses English in a new way to capture the tropical vibrancy of an important but neglected heritage of English-speaking peoples; William Oxley, a distinguished example of a poet who through a commitment to extending the modernist project has been set somewhat outside the mainstream, which speaks poorly for the mainstream; and the really excellent Sophie Hannah, a sort of hip, 90s Stevie Smith whose talent for pointed and polished wit also embodies an older, specifically English tradition which goes right back to Dryden. There is also Jeremy Young, whose verses show how good academic poetry might have been if it had not been left to the Academics; and Peter Mortimer, whose vigorous fancy is an inheritance of the specifically 1960's beat and hip incarnations of modernism. And there is Matt Simpson, whose scouse dialect poems are attractively muscular, and who can be impressive in some of his working-man's slice of life pieces, which suggest a sort of Philip Larkin of the docks. These poets are clearly a very mixed lot, but they all, I think, share in one way or another a commitment to reviving and extending the true tradition. If we combine the loyal independence of this eclectic group with the street-wise curiosity of the City Kids and the tough and bracing winds blowing from the north, we can see that behind the domesticated facade of verse which official taste has enshrined in commercial and academic respectability, there exists a contemporary British poetry which is as energetic, ambitious, diverse, and morally serious as it has ever been in its long and splendid history.[1]

[1] An earlier version of this paper was delivered by invitation at the University of Salzburg's 1996 conference on Contemporary British and Irish Poetry in the Making, and appears in the conference's *Proceedings*. For their help in researching this essay, and with no implication that they necessarily endorse the opinions or the judgements on individual poets expressed in it, I would like to thank Fred Beake, Douglas Clark and Tim Love.

Aonghas Macneacail

When a smile leaves its host

when a smile leaves its host
when it becomes detached from the lips
when it vacates the dark heart of the eyes
no longer crouches on the upper brae of the cheeks
goes gliding off along those ordered
avenues those shimmering promenades arcades
and all the brittle back streets
flitting between highlights and shadows
keeping its definition to itself
swoops soars and bursts into a kind of
genially predatory song of fluting fiddling
kindles multitudes to dig life from a drum
those who should mistake its transport
for an ordinary rage or joy may find it
necessary to reconstruct themselves
the eye must learn to read the meaning in
a smile that branches out on its own trail
the ear must cut a new path clear between
old sympathies contentments
this is a wild unpredictable being now
it may ogle fondle flirt caress
in the wrong humour rake
the face of convention it might leap
stark naked into baptismal pools
intoxicated with its own liquidity
for liberty no smile has ever been so rich
can be swan or swallow shark or salmon
may decide to take root and spread great
leafy branches out across the world
become a berry-laden cup or
nestle catlike private on its hearth
it will build its contrary resilience
into a bulwark against weathers
it will seek converts it cannot
live alone for long

Sùisinis 1996

i, present here, alone
have human breath to
offer sùisinis
this pale gray afternoon
the wind is silent, elsewhere,
over there the sea's asleep, the
cuillin's great saw masked, but
here, where there were
ceilidhs, quarrels, courtships, still
the mason's measured art remains
while hearths are air-conditioned,
thatch and thatcher long absorbed
into the turf, the singing wheel
which spans at summer doors
is air, is memory, the stories
of old voyages, from
lochlann and from gaelic south
which married here, have long since
put on threadbare coats and left,
those tweeds which took their colours
from the rocks and leaves did not
go willingly, their dumb inheritors
(still numerous) have nothing much to say –
a cough, a bleat, a cropped appraisal
of sweet grass, shrugged fleece, while
there an eyeless shepherd's house
still wears its iron hat, red, furrowed, dropping
rust into a skewed and swollen mattress
which sinks through the broken bed as if
a ship of scaffolding gone down were
dragging this dark porous reef, its nemesis
and as I walk among stone vacancies
the ghosts I call on stay indoors, while
on these shaven grazings, *any questions*
from my pocket radio discusses "bovine
spongiform encephalopathy" and how
it's cheaper to feed blood and bone
to herbivores

A pathology of the normal

one day, your breath
will cease
to be an issue

some hopes you have

some hopes you have of
climbing to the summit on
that narrow road pockmarked
with thorns and you don't
know yet the shape of it
that ultimate peak that pap
of air and this is not
the plane you thought you'd
be on if in films the big star
reaches out to grasp
an overhang, immune
to falling shards of
murderous geologies out
here there is only that bare
sour-buttered lip of rock
you balance on the wind
while swollen violins run
trilling fingers through
your knotted hair and as
you lean into that airborne
pause
      then fall

(vermeer's exact) note
how your shirt now filled
and billowed doesn't
slow your plummet

let that abattoir earth
growing toward you be
      sheer dream

The need to nest is always there

by being
other than you are
you live
in places such as this
that's not
not home

and being here
you sometimes feel your
whole i.d.
is
up for grabs

and even when you've settled
with your hook, your lexicon
of manageable definitions
there's always yet another
small unnameable unease
a storm
remains within the seed

that tip on the grand

it's a bit
of
a hard luck story, too

take a phrase like
more or less,
          why
does it always know
exactly where to come
between for example
the winning nag
and
the yellow betting slip you
rip and rip and rip

how a birthplace is remembered

there's an island there
and a wee star in it
a radiance of
singing brightly
raw silk woven into lace

there's a firmament
of grass and gabbro
where light is flesh
tall beacons on their feet
still glittering

a breath of stone
insists that tides will
harmonise this shore's
i am with all earth's
deep and widest smiles

light

finally, there is light at the end of this long slow corridor of months. a grey sky begins to peel back, begins to clean. it's like a folding away of dark blankets, an unfolding of clear light sheets. the streetlights, glistening like a yellow hoar-frost on the distant brae, look out of place, nonplussed a little, though the slopes they rest on seem, from here, in here, quite dark

behind are footfalls, in the shade, not following. one reader of the darkness pads away, leaves silence, other motions swell from tap to clatter, loud across that open vein behind, then fade, diminuendo. a pair of brogues shape heavy echoes left to right, stilettoes quick-step from right to left. no voices walk. the corridor's a whisper yet to bud. a cataract that draws the eyes back into all the tumbling absences, its maze

this is the choice. there are no choices. the corridor will be returned to, entered into. for the moment and for growth, that mouth that leads to air and ligth comes first

lost dog – but

she's down there somewhere tracking rabbits or
she's with a hopeful suitor (hopeless, really) either
way, this canine centenarian virgin is not listening to any
whistle, call, entreaty, threat – at midnight, dark, the stars
are flickering pinholes in the black silk fabric of a proximate
sky, the fields, beyond this tangible underfoot, are absences
the trees are sounds like restless voices she is not
at home, not in the skeletal garden, nor caught in torchbeam
as we pan across foreshortened ridges, furrows she's not
anywhere that time-charred weathered treestump's
not a dog, although its writhing shape and though we
whistle, call, cajole, although we yell her name in voices
interbreeding (well past bedtime) petulance and care, she's
just not there to go into the woods would be to lose
all sense (this shadowy time of night) of space, direction –
but see, beyond those fields are folds of sleeping sheep –
too much at ease, she *can't* be there – she never could
decide between her hunting and her herding gene
again we circumnavigate the inner field, we call, we
aim our torchbeam at a shadow – it's a shadow but
away below, toward the house, we hear a puppish *yip*
it's dog, it's saying *let me in* – and we're not in. not yet –
not, laughing, yet

Loveable Warts
A Defence of Self-Indulgence

Neil K Henderson

Two most frequently aired criticisms of new writing are lack of originality and self-indulgence. In a sense, these are opposite extremes of the same problem: trying to express timeless human preoccupations in apparently novel and interesting variations. If the writer leans too much towards his peers or predecessors, he is not 'original'; if he becomes too much of a slave to his own whims and foibles, he is 'self-indulgent'.

Taking the first sin first: what do we mean by 'originality' anyway? Surely this indicates some totally new conception; coming up with an idea, form, viewpoint, or situation which has never *ever* 'been done' before. To *originate* is to *beget* - to create for the *very first time*. Now, how many thousands of years is it since the cave paintings of Altamira and Lascaux were made? In all that time, the art of painting seems to have gone through every conceivable permutation of colour, form, texture and style – from the wildest abstraction to the most authentic representation. And there has doubtless been a mighty legion of 'originators' who have initiated major advances in sundry directions, as the evolution of art progressed – not to mention the myriad of minor innovators and mere imitators who followed after them. So I rather suspect that, by this late dog-end of modernity, there will be precious little 'originating' left to do. The human eye has its limitations, after all. Opportunities for breaking new ground, however plentiful at first, must ultimately prove *finite*.

The same goes with writing: surely the human consciousness must have long ago reached the full extent of its capacity for true inventiveness. Not that there's any harm in *trying* to be original – but if this is the sole criterion, the results are hardly likely to ooze artistic integrity. Again, if we delude ourselves that we have actually achieved something *unique*, then time is likely to knock us off our ivory pedestal, disclosing an ancient and revered family tree for 'our' invention, stretching back to the primeval runic notebook. Who hasn't nurtured that special pet notion for half eternity, waiting for the perfect moment to spring it on a grateful public, only to discover that it has not only been done before - but *famously* and *successfully?* God knows, every time I catch my face in the morning mirror, I curse Mary Shelley for beating me to it . . .

As it is, I think most of us must be content with 'doing our own thing' in the knowledge that there isn't likely to be anything earth-shatteringly new to say – though there are infinite possibilities of variety in modes of expression, subtleties of insight, and so forth. Just as human beings are infinitely varied, while very few individuals stand out as being really exceptional.

Returning to *Frankenstein* (and the same applies to *Jekyll and Hyde* or *Confessions of a Justified Sinner*) – there would seem to be a limitless potential for re-inventing the general metaphor stemming from the original work. Without being truly 'original' themselves, new interpreters yet have infinite scope for *individuality* of expression. (And how 'original' were the original authors? Mrs Shelley had *Genesis* to draw upon, as Stevenson had Deacon Brodie and Hogg had Scottish religious fanaticism.) But, short of Divine Inspiration, full-blown originality would appear to be in scant supply. Of course, I'm not saying there is *nothing* original left to do – the whole point of innovation is that you can't see it coming, so anything might still be possible.

It is worth remembering here that 'originality' has only come to be regarded as a virtue in comparatively recent times. The likes of Chaucer and Shakespeare (or Henryson and Dunbar) made no secret of their use of earlier sources. The provenance of a story had to be traceable to some undisputed authority from the past. You didn't get much credit for just 'making it up', when *fiction* was synonymous with *lies*. And, depending on the religious climate, questions of 'bearing false witness' – or even demonic possession – might arise from overenthusiastic displays of original thinking. More than anything, it would be a writer's skill in putting his stuff across to the reader, using – or in spite of – the rigid literary conventions of the time, which would determine the level of his popular 'success'. In other words: it was the singer, not the song. (One modern singer who has successfully reverted to this 'informed by authority' attitude of earlier writers, is Hugh MacDiarmid, who – as in *To a Friend and Fellow Poet* – has bodily lifted passages of scientific text with which to argue his artistic cause, to startling effect. This might be seen as an original use of un-original material.)

But this focus on the singer before the song brings us round to the significance of *personality*, as reflected in a writer's style – which is where the horned toad of *self-indulgence* might be expected to lurk, impatient to start scuttling about aimlessly, should the stone of self-restraint be ever-so-slightly lifted. And would that really be so terrible? Maybe, after all, our toad can be made to metamorphose into a charming young aristocrat – given some judicial TLC by its author . . .

Now, a writer's personality can impress itself on his work in more than one way. On a superficial level, he may be letting his unguarded self spill over onto the page – which is certainly an immediate source of that 'individuality' which I have mentioned. If this is done carelessly – and especially if it is detrimental to the writing – then it can be classed as self-indulgence. Whether or not this is seen as 'bad', however, must surely depend on how attractive that personality is in itself, and what our motives are in reading him. Take McGonagall. He is probably more popular now than he has ever been, though it would be hard to find a more glaring example of single-minded self-indulgence in defiance of every standard of 'quality'. I daresay much of his appeal stems from sympathy with the underdog, mingled with posthumous patronage – but I also believe that he is regarded with affection as a loveable eccentric. An *individualist*, in fact. His work may be held in derision, but *he* – as a *personality* – continues to be read. Indeed, he has even been described by one critic as "the only truly memorable bad poet". Whatever the reason, his work gives pleasure and his fame lives on.

Of course, a writer may bring his personality to the fore without incurring charges of self-indulgence. An ability to portray one's idiosyncratic verbal mannerisms honestly and without affectation is, after all, a valuable stylistic attribute very difficult to cultivate. On the other hand, some writers introduce their 'real' selves into the plot, as fleshed-out characters. This has got to be self-indulgence, almost by definition, but it can nevertheless prove most effective in some cases. (*The French Lieutenant's Woman* and *Slaughterhouse-Five* spring to mind.)

But when it comes to self-advertisement, what could be more indulgent than Sir Walter Scott's trumpet-blowing in *Waverley?* Chapter XXIV opens: "Shall this be a long or a short chapter?— This is a question in which you, gentle reader, have no vote, however much you may be interested in the consequences . . ." Well no-one can say we haven't been warned. The gentle reader is then treated to a prodigious display of dithering with detail, and a quoted verse, before the Learned Author promises to proceed in his story "with all the brevity that my natural style of composition, partaking of what scholars call the periphrastic and ambigatory, and the vulgar the circumbendibus, will permit me." That's his style, reader, and he's sticking to it. And I can't help admiring the candour with which he upholds his "natural style" for what it is.

It has been said that the most successful writer keeps himself completely in the background. This may hold true if all we want is the sterile perfection of establishment-approved proficiency. For myself, though, I can't consider a work to be *artistically* successful – in the widest sense – unless it has a 'soul'. And who provides that, if not the artist? Give me soul food at the expense of 'merit', every time. After all, where is the merriment in mere aesthetics? Intellectual self-repression may win prestigious prizes, while Scott's grandiose apostrophising is destined for the Wart-Book of Posterity, but if it ain't got a soul, who cares if it's smooth as silk?

This 'soul' doesn't need to be magnificent and all-embracing – just so long as it's *there*. One of the most depressingly soulless forms of self-indulgent writing is the kind where the author amuses himself playing 'clever' word games, from which the reader is excluded unless he can crack some esoteric 'code'. I call this the 'crossword puzzle' school of literature, which may appeal to the academic problem-solving mentality. Conversely, in some cases – like MacDiarmid's poem 'Water Music' – lists of obscure terms are arranged in such a way as to provide their own 'soul' through the music of their sound value alone. Such sincere artistic endeavours can hardly be called self-indulgent, but while the reader's innate 'code-cracking' faculties must inevitably interfere with the sonic word-flow, there is the risk that the 'logopoeia' will counteract the 'melopoeia', inviting the charge of 'lagomorphia' (i.e. 'rabbiting on').

In a lighter vein, it is possible for a writer to introduce playful elements largely for the entertainment of himself and friends – therefore as a self-indulgence - without detracting from the artistic worth of the whole: Lewis

Carroll's *Alice* books being a case in point. It is known that Dodgson was fond of peppering his works with in-jokes and parodies (often at his own expense) for the benefit of his Oxford colleagues and their families, even making oblique references to certain mathematical theories that tickled his fancy. Now, almost a hundred years after his death, the majority of these allusions are lost upon the modern reader. But, far from marring the enjoyment of the stories, the inclusion of these self-indulgences serves to *enhance* and *enrich* them by an added dimension of 'inner reality' imparting to the nonsense that 'nearly sense' which makes it so effective. Once again, we come back to that elusive element 'soul'. It is the pervasive spirit of Charles Lutwidge Dodgson, with his delights and dalliances, which makes his magic *live*. Indeed, it is precisely this 'self-indulgent' quality which distinguishes the work as a true labour of love.

If we follow this line of thought yet further, we can see how the playful aspect of self-indulgence can take over completely – to the extent of becoming the entire *raison d'etre* of a creative endeavour. Look at *The Goon Show*. I think it is fair to say that this legendary paragon of performance art could not have existed at all *without* self-indulgence. And yet, far from arousing censure, the incessant in-jokes, inconsequential ramblings and scarcely existing plot, the endlessly repeated funny noises and aimless wanderings to and from the script, have been applauded and marvelled at from the fifties to the present day. Here, I think one must admit, lurks something that looks like *originality*, after all. At least, it has a very strongly developed individualist streak. And, of course, the great-souled personality of Spike Milligan is the omnipresent life-force of the experience. So much so, that we come to regard the show as a *person* in its own right – making allowances for its imperfections as we would overlook the carbuncles on the kisser of a much-loved friend. (Perhaps our horned toad will make it to the ball yet . . .)

So far, I have been concentrating on one specific type of self-indulgence: that is, creative or 'positive' self-indulgence. Even so, I would only claim a qualified defence of it. I am not trying to advocate it as a necessary criterion – any more than I would advocate the quest for 'originality' as an end in itself. What I *am* saying is that a *degree* of self-indulgence in the creative process is likely to result in work of a more honestly individual, unpredictable and memorable – yes, even sometimes *loveable* – nature: warts 'n' all. Some things might be better without the warts, but maybe the thought processes involved in attempting to eradicate them can in turn lead to yet more innovative discoveries along the way.

One of my own warty indulgences involves knitting together dreams and private thought associations, so that newly discovered chains of 'logic' can be followed to surprising and intriguing conclusions. And a conclusion need not be at the end of a story. Despite the dictates of the beginning-middle-and-end tradition, I prefer to think of a narrative as consisting of two ends: the Writer End and the Reader End. During the creative process, something extra-dimensional happens. The writer may achieve something far beyond his original conception. The reader may interpret the finished work from his own perspective or experience, in a way wholly unintended by the author. Thus, whichever end you start from, the piece can turn out to be a Surprising Conclusion *in its entirety*.

Any kind of experimental or exploratory writing may be considered self-indulgent by its very rationale. Purists will no doubt state that the duty of the writer is to communicate as clearly and directly as he can with his reader, who is not to be used as a literary guinea-pig. This is where I claim immunity on the grounds of 'art'. An artist owes it to himself to remain true to his initial vision, wherever it may lead him. I believe that creativity is about exploring, discovering, re-evaluating, adapting – and whether or not there is such a thing as 'progress' in the arts in general, the work of the individual artist is constantly evolving throughout his lifetime. Self-indulgence (including mistakes) is a means to evolutionary diversity – just as, in nature, some 'freak' development like a long neck or a colour that frightens predators can turn out to be of vital importance to the species, yet would not have come to light if 'standard practice' had been rigidly adhered to.

So much for 'positive' self-indulgence. It might be as well to look at 'negative' self-indulgence here – if only to eliminate it from our defence. This is how a writer can achieve stylistic individuality for all the wrong reasons, like McGonagall. Certainly, the kind of self-indulgence which results in sloppy or unreadable work cannot seriously be condoned - but who among us hasn't cut the odd corner at some time? Who hasn't yielded to pressure of deadlines or mounting workload with the justification: "It'll have to go out the way it is, or not at all – the next one will be better"? (I don't think *I'll* be casting the first stone . . .)

Then there's the sin of leaving that little bit in because you "like the look of it" – even though it's clearly surplus to requirements. 'Poetic licence' might be a suitable get-out clause here. Does everything *have* to have a recognisable 'function' within a piece of writing? Can't something peculiar be put in, just on the off-chance that a Surprise Conclusion may be reached at the Reader End – possibly at a far-off date? Don't our disenchanted descendents deserve something truly *trivial* against which to measure the weighty po-facedness of Heavy Pre-Millennium Literature? Maybe Wally Scott's grandiose digressions will come to be highly valued - his stories seen as mere vehicles for their preservation. It depends whether there is more interest in people than in story-telling – because this kind of self-indulgence gives a glimpse of the human behind the narrative 'voice'.

How can we be sure that our early ancestors were any more self-disciplined when they created their vast murals on the cave walls of Europe? Perhaps a palaeolithic Brian Sewell was standing at the back, complaining about some 'unnecessary' inclusion we can't now recognise. But we accept the work in its existing form. And *we* call it *Art*. (Though maybe, after all, our present notion of self-indulgence only relates to more sophisticated modes of expression.)

Some 'negative' self-indulgences are defended on the grounds of promoting 'realism' over 'stylisation'. There is the current trend for abandoning all forms of punctuation, especially in poetry. I think e e cummings cornered the market in eccentric punctuation – so any claim to 'originality' can rest with him. But, while I can concede a social/ educational levelling value, I take the cynical view that the unpunctuated mode is adopted for two equally dubious reasons: (a) it's easier to type in a hurry, and (b) it saves lazy writers having to check for 'correct' usage. I'm not saying that we should all sit for two days, like Flaubert, agonising over a comma, but some writers ought to realise that judicious use of conventional punctuation actually makes things *easier to read*, and therefore greatly aids the writer in getting his intentions across.

Having said this, I must add that I don't believe it to be incumbent on the creative artist to deviate from the path dictated by his own integrity simply to make life easier for his audience. Lazy reading habits are a passive form of self-indulgence in themselves. (Oh, look – an unruly horned toad has just swallowed up a literary guinea-pig!) Sometimes, however, a compromise has to be reached, as with verse in English containing peculiarly Scottish rhymes. While the author may not wish to modify his work for a non-Scottish audience, some form of annotation will at least reduce misunderstanding.

Of course, ultimately the writer aims to achieve the perfect balance of artistic faithfulness and clear communication. But before doing so, he will doubtless have grown through, and out of, his own personal set of productive peccadillos. I am forever having to re-learn the lesson that puns are not inventions – they merely lie there in the language, available for use by whoever happens along. This means thousands of people before me. However, if the habit is allowed to burn itself out naturally, intriguing new concepts can be unearthed, which may provide fuel for further invention beyond the initial wordplay. The important thing is to let go of the old stock, once something better materialises.

As it is, I can only defend self-indulgence up to a point. Writing is work, after all – for those who want to be taken seriously. Yet it continues to be a learning process, no matter how well practised we become. And what more natural way to learn than through play? While we play we discover our strengths and weaknesses, and develop a personality of our own. All work and no play, and Jack might become just a tired old cliché. On the other hand, there is always the possibility of something wonderfully unexpected, just out of sight, waiting to be discovered by a happy accident. Who knows – maybe some day we might even do something *original* . . .

Roger Caldwell

Dark Ages

The old man died. It wasn't simple
though he made it as simple as dying may be.
Hard to believe, he spoke so quiet, straight
for one in pain, that day we knew a saint.
For myself, who lack all sanctity, or hope
of any better place, and scornful of a worse,
I shall go howling, can't, and won't, forgive
my enemies. It seems this man had none.

Not aspiring, wishing to be saints ourselves,
we were grateful to have known a saint.
We've returned to brawling and the ale-bench now,
but the oars were silent and the sea was calm
when we placed his body on the boat
and rowed it across to Lindisfarne.

To Alexander (With Apologies)

I've put aside my childish toys.
To him they're all he has.

I love silence, solitude and thought.
To him that's death.

His world and mine should never meet.
He makes damned sure they do.

He doesn't see I scorn his infant's ways,
his puerile pursuits.

Yet perhaps the day will come
when he'll examine how I spent my time

– "Such rubbish was it
that you wasted life on?" –

and, having long outgrown his toys,
laughs at me who couldn't outgrow mine.

And I'd no right to show disdain
at a child's penny-farthing brain.

It's I who stand in the schoolroom corner
in a dunce's cap and, on a slate,

analphabetic, try to write
while God and time look grimly on.

Not Yet Avila

Strange solitudes. On this parched plain
all's turned to shadows where no shadows lie.
And this is not Avila. Dusty roads
know heat intenser than Castilian heat,
lack shade before the blinded eye
where most the demons, devils play

– I snap my fingers at them, unafraid.
But they shall be afraid of me.
It was said, a mere woman, I had no rights –
No more a man has. In the Prayer of Quiet
what came unsummoned you could not control
nor put the sun out, stop the daybreak.

Here each fortaleza more confines oneself
and I feel like a bird with a broken wing.
I find such loneliness in spiritual matters.
Indeed I find loneliness everywhere.
Doctora mística, the Inquisition's books
were ignorant of God "among the pots and pans".

And the angel came, and in his hands
a golden spear which seemed to pierce my heart.
And when at last he drew it out
I was burning with the love of God.
Ludus amoris, endgame stratagems
we use to checkmate the Divine King

– to be united in a loving kiss
asleep to the world, not knowing if
the body still has life to breathe
when neither hands nor feet can move,
the eyes, if open, seeing nothing
that have seen the Castle's inmost room.

But here is not Avila. There's no Wound of Love,
Transverberation of the Heart. Eighteen,
I wandered out from Zaragoza on into
the hot interior. Strange solitudes instead,
Teresa, and decades on a dusty road.
Yet your destination wasn't out of reach.

Rain fell somewhere on a quiet stream
to mingle after miles with open sea,
and across that vast expanse of water
you made your ocean-voyage to "eternity".
Far inland I find driftwood now.
No rain as yet. No angel comes.

Legend

The day was chosen for the sacrifice.
The sea was sated but demanded more.
Three girls were chosen to pay the price
who had done nothing to be sorry for.

As they were led down to the beach in chains
all of the townsmen shouted and waved
and never a thought was in their brains
but: "You are finished, and we are saved."

At the sea's edge were three great stones.
One of the girls to each was bound
and left to the beach's whitened bones,
and waves which broke with a mocking sound.

The townsmen were feasting far away.
Like the waves their music rose and fell.
The sea slide further into the bay.
The monster rose from the depths of hell

with hungry sea-green eyes which stared
on humankind so young and slim,
the vulnerable sweet flesh bared,
and came where they awaited him,

and said: "The slimy seaweed clings.
It's like a hand which throttles me.
Who cares what fish-tailed sea-hag sings?
I could not grow to love the sea,

and salt-tears were the tears I shed.
Indeed, I found no comfort there.
I come to try the land instead."
And wiped his fingers in their golden hair.

Illustration by David Stephenson

Maurice Lindsay

Kissing Earth

The Pope, that ancient celibate,
seems strangely sure of women's needs,
losing no chance to preach and prate
unfettered married sex that breeds.
No matter how we cultivate
blind faith, it's tending fertile seeds
with husbandry to generate
what triumphs over fertile weeds
keeps piety in pomp and state
to spider monkish man-made creeds
with fancied after-life for bait.
Unstarving death is all he feeds.

A Calling Card

Allow me to introduce myself. I'm God's
unpleasant side; like Him, by you created
to even up, I'd guess, the boring odds
goodness and pleasured ease might leave you sated.
I'm black-as-painted; coin's reverse; hid moon
as earth spins doubly round its axis pole –
midnight for others while for some, high noon –
the conscience pricking your imagined soul:
the heart of what my opposite gave you; choice
to torture, cheat, make wars with fractured laws;
like Him, a silent fancied inner voice,
though I don't seek perpetual applause.
What you are here for, where faith claims you'll go,
how in the name of Hell am I to know?

Greyhound

He'd covered years of distance, winning races
that often breasted home the fleeted gains
of betting, pounding round those breathless lanes
where other greyhounds strained for faster paces;
was roughly fondled down his narrow ears,
not with affection, but because each prize
made him in his beloved owner's eyes
a cause for boasting over paid-for beers.
Until, one day, electric hares moved faster
than heart and legs could gain upon. Out running
beside the town's canal, picked up and thrown
into the water by his worshipped master
and held beneath with struggled senses stunning,
a jogger hearing: *Drown, you bastard, drown.*

LANGHOLM AND ESKDALE
MUSIC AND ARTS FESTIVAL

POETRY IN ESKDALE

Monday 25 August 1997, Eskdale Hotel,
Langholm, Dumfriesshire 8.00 p.m.

Poems and Pints

John Hudson: Poet, Editor and Screenplay Writer
Tom Pow: Poet, Teacher, Travel Writer, Radio Presenter
Chrys Salt: Poet, Artistic Director, Broadcaster

****

Tickets £3.00 each

****

Friday 29 August 1997, Eskdale Hotel,
Langholm, Dumfriesshire 8.00 p.m.

Hugh MacDiarmid in Verse and Song

with *Dr. Jamie Reid Baxter* presenting a celebration of
Hugh MacDiarmid as a poet of the Scottish Borders.With
tenor *Wills Morgan* and baritone *Andrew Doig*
accompanied by pianist *Richard Black*.

****

Tickets £4.00 each

****

For further information telephone Festival Office at 01387 80914 or
Tourist Information Office at 01387 80976.

Inside out

G A Pickin

It was brilliant, standing in the queue. We'd gone to the pub for a good half hour before, then we'd stopped at the off licence for some cans of Tennent's to fortify the camaraderie. Someone started 'Flower of Scotland', and we all joined in. Like I said, it was brilliant.

I must be one of the few Englishmen who knows all the verses, not just the football supporters' version. I reckon I'm an honorary Scot, if I do say so myself. I vote SNP, I went on all the Poll Tax protests, I celebrate Hogmanay, St Andrew's Day, and Burns Night. I draw the line at bagpipes and haggis, but there are plenty of my mates here who feel the same. Being Scots isn't about antiquated customs and some quaint dialectic phrases spoken in broad accents, it's a state of mind. It took me a little while to suss it out. Like most of my countrymen I was thrown off the scent by the usual decoys – the Loch Ness Monster, tartan trousers and Oor Willie – but I got there in the end. The crux of true Scots lies in being anti-English.

'Down with White Settlers!' I shouted, and they all echoed, my mate Robert bashing me on the arm and laughing with his whole body, the way only Glaswegians can. He's an incomer here himself; we came down when we finished at college to get the boat from Stranraer over to Belfast for a swift holiday, and ended up working on the ferries. It's a good laugh most of the time, and the money's decent, even if the shifts are a pig sometimes.

As soon as the news came out that the arts centre was going to show *Braveheart*, a gang of us from the Downshire decided we'd all go together and make a real event of it. All the reviews said it was a great version of the William Wallace story, complete with a realistic disembowelling at the end. Never mind that Mel Gibson's accent was a bit dodgy, or that the producers had chosen Ireland over Scotland as a more realistic-looking location for filming, this was the inspiring tale of a working-class Scotsman defying the bastard English against all odds. Perfect.

Up ahead, the cashier was giving Tom a hard time about the tickets, not wanting to let a bunch of rowdies in to spoil things for everyone else. I stepped forward and put on the charm. "Come on, love, this is what the film's all about. The Scottish spirit of independence, 'Rise and be a nation again', and all that. We won't cause bother once the film's started – we're just being patriotic."

"I can tell you're not from round here", was all she said, but she gave us the tickets in the end, and they all congratulated me.

We sat in the front row. Before I took my seat, I turned round and had a look to see if anyone else knew I was here. I could see my brother Mike sitting smack in the middle with his girlfriend Pat. They were talking with their heads close together, looking dead serious. My brother doesn't know what fun is, but then, he's never fitted in the way I have. If you ask me, he's always trying too hard – learning Gaelic, and Scots, spending half the time with his nose in yet another tome on Culloden or the Highland Clearances. He's always *apologising* for being English – even Pat gets sick of it, and tells him just to be his own person.

Like me. Being accepted is learning to laugh at yourself – out-Scots the Scots. It's all about Irn-Bru and Billy Connolly and the Dark Island. I'm one of the crowd, all right. There's nobody would deny that.

The film's starting now, and soon we're all into it, watching Mel outsmart the pompous, corrupt English, overcoming even the treachery of his own side (all upper-class turncoats, of course). There's one scene where this Irish geezer comes up to Mel and tells him he wants to fight alongside him for the Scottish cause. Mel tries to put him off by telling him about the odds, but he's not bothered about any of that. He asks "If I join up with you, do I get to kill Englishmen"? When Mel says yes, the whole cinema cheers like they'd been given the go ahead to do just that themselves.

Robert takes a sly look in my direction to see how I'm taking it, but, I'm shouting louder than the rest. He laughs and slaps my arm dead hard, and I pretend to hang myself, tongue lolling out, cross-eyed. I turn round in my seat again, to see how my brother is taking all this death-to-the-Sassenach stuff. Pat is looking at him like Robert looked at me, worried in case he feels offended, but instead of letting her know that he understands, he's sitting there all stony-faced, staring at the screen real hard as if it might make him invisible to the blood-thirsty crowd. It's so pathetic, I almost want to stand up and point to him, shouting to the cinema:

"Here's one right here. Come and get the bastard, he'd sell you down the river as soon as look at you!" But I don't, of course. Still it would serve him right.

We settle down again to watch these really mega battle scenes, and old Mel just gets braver and more audacious as the film goes on. The ending is brilliant, where the executioner offers him a quick merciful death if he'll denounce Scottish freedom, which, naturally, he refuses to do.

A hush falls over the whole cinema when he gets disembowelled, and remains quiet, a mark of respect almost, as we watch Robert the Bruce come to his senses and decide to take up the cause. The silence remains as the credits roll. Then lights come on, and the crowd slowly shakes itself into the real world. People keeping their voices low, filing out in an orderly way, without the usual pushing and shoving.

I jump up, invigorated, pulling on my coat. I turn to Robert and start to make some joke about being lynched in the car park if anyone hears my accent, but stop dead in my tracks when I see his face. Robert, big, tough Glaswegian Robert, is crying. Actually crying, with great tears rolling down his cheeks.

"He's not really dead", I grin, trying to cheer him up,."They use micro-surgery to sew his guts back in and he opens a chip shop in Newton Stewart".

Robert stares at me, a look that's annoyed, hurt, and hostile all the same time. "You don't understand", he says, in this flat, peculiar voice.

"Sure I do. He's a hero, absolutely brilliant. He's ..."

"You can't understand. What he meant, what we've lost . . ." He turned away from me and walked towards the door, his back defying me to follow and disturb him. Confused, I let him walk away, then I turn and search the crowd for my brother. I can see him and Pat coming down the side aisle. She's crying as well, and, instead of putting his arm around her, like I would have done, he's walking a little behind her, like an acquaintance at a funeral, respectful, clumsy, and out of place.

"Hey, Mike, it was brilliant, wasn't it? That part where they blitz York . . ."

"Shut up, John", he says in that low, I'll-kill-you-when-we-get-home, voice. And he pushes past me like I was some drunken tramp blocking the door to the church, for Christsakes, and goes after Pat, who's hurrying stiff-shouldered through the exit.

The cinema is empty. The house lights show up the sweetie wrappers and empty fag packets dropped between the rows, which look dishevelled as well, with some seats up while others are still pushed down. The silence has returned after the shuffling of the exiting crowd, but this isn't a respectful silence, just an empty one.

It's there too outside in the car park, this silence. I can't see any of the lads, not even Robert, who never goes anywhere without me. I guess he expects me to meet him in the Downshire, where we can rehash all the goriest bits, reciting our favourite lines, maybe have a bit of a sing-song. I rehearse in my head how we'll replay that scene with the Irishman, milking it for all it's worth.

But something tells me that tonight's not the night. It's not that I wouldn't be welcome; hell, I know they'll miss me. Robert's always saying I'm the life and soul, but . . . I don't know. There was something about Robert's face, his voice, that just makes me think a night in on my own wouldn't go amiss. I'll just have to save it up for tomorrow. Yeah, I'll save it all till tomorrow when the whole gang of us will be travelling up for the Rangers v. Celtic match. We'll have the coach rocking with our songs and chants – and my voice will be the loudest of all.

It'll be brilliant.

Sally Evans

Circular Weather Girl Poem

She probes the wintry weather, her voice oiled
and golden, warns of the violet-hued storm,
reports the deluge flooding yard and lawn
like a spring haiku thawing icicles.
She points to where the cherry blossoms fall
that still lie wrapped in cherry leaves, the wall
waiting to be hidden by leaf and blob.

A goddess, or a sort of priest with sisters
she waves away the Atlantic squall: she deals
in chance percentages of rainy blusters
born in the doldrums, off Biscay or Faroe.
Her every isobar travels through a spring
of butterflies – Gauguin dreams, Pissaro
or Botticelli Floras riding bicycles.

She is the weather girl, our newest myth,
our crowned queen, Cinderella, our blind date.
She came to life when Barbie dolls in moonlight
had lesbian affairs with women graduates.
The cherry blossom looks like rags; but pigeons
and rooks wait for those cherries; in their religions
her pumpkin riches can't be marred or spoiled.

She probes the wintry weather, her voice oiled.

The Young American Walking the Coastline

There he was, at the campsite breakfast,
the young American walking the coastline,
pack and boots, jeans and cap,
eating his toast before the day's lap
of cliff, coast, road and beach.

The warden, between fixing eggburgers
on a spitting stove at the bar,
asked him how many weeks last year
he had taken to trail the seascapes –
for this was his second trek, via Thurso
to Ayrshire from Inverness.

Yes, we smiled, we're from Scotland.
From Edinburgh, yes it's nice –
but the tourists go round the castle, not us –
we don't walk the coastline twice.
We caught sight of him, tiny and grand
as we sped past on the coast road,

wondering, confusingly, whether it's best
to walk round Scotland from East or West –
whether set to the morning or evening sun.
You never know what an American will do next,
we added, thinking all morning of this young man,

as he piled Scotland into his rucksack,
his face as weathered as the rocks,
mesmerised by the forest,
a captive of the open shore,
counting the uncontrollable headlands
and racing the unbeatable sun.

Motorway with Owl and Geese

A motorway, overwhelmed at dawn
by thousands of geese unwinding their skeins

on fields of translucent white, tea-leaves
to stir a storm, doodlebugs thudding

on pilgrimages to Ireland and Mourne,
whose wings beat three feet

above the warned wave of cobles
coasting the migration morning

of international geese, where our dawn
crosses under theirs.

A day on, our southward return
against the enticing rhythmic moon

setting a pace for language in its field-wise face
and the swing of strong wings –

the white owl lobs through the darkness,
past cars' predictable pale darts

correcting the motorway's passive, unattended
calendar, its clock of ghosts.

After Tagore's Garden

After Tagore's Garden I walked in my own garden.
After Sorley Maclean's Wood I wandered in my own
and there were paths in the garden and woods.

Their magnificent garden and woods were not foreign
but bustling and bursting with blossom and bay
in other languages carried my breath away.

Demanding, spellbound I followed. A cloud lifted
revealing a horizon high as Muir's Grove view.
My balance shifted; clearly I climbed back from peril.

I climbed slowly round MacDiarmid, stone wobbling,
from Stevie in delirium, Yeats in recovery,
to dear American Frost (I lost Pounds).

Scots and Welsh balladry read in their first tongues,
placed in my English garden, flourished there,
and when I transplanted that garden to Scotland
I was glad Gawain and Chaucer already grew there.

I have made an English garden in Scotland.
That is what the gods demanded of me.
It is more and more reliably my own.
Once inside, it is not terrifying.

Neither is it inside, exactly. It is on a fell,
in the North of England one minute, the next at Amulree,
then it sneaks to London or Italy

but mostly, it is a Scottish garden. I demand
dual nationality. I have gained it by marrying Scotland,
and at that, marrying for love. I have earned it with words.

Here are the flowers, hot and open. Here are its shrubs
and here is a piscina, or fish-pond (Latin) and a pergola (Greek)
and a tree. An old English word. Oh my friends
of the yard, garth, garden, earth, allow me to be
as my language continues it linking
growth in my garden, wishing to see

from its found view, Raasay and Rabindranath
sharing their plants like flourishing leaves
where everything draws nourishment
from the great trees turning on yesterday.
On soil of the past, we stir and water the present
in the warmth of our languages, grow, not shrinking
from our gardens, forward, free.

Zeus

Phidias made me. I live.
Ivory and gold, I give
of the Aegean belief
the living live to achieve.
You should not come to grief.

Throned in my temple,
knees and limbs powerful
through the Olympian fight
by the best of your kind
beautiful and upright,

I sit like a language,
am told of, a tale,
am sung of, a legend
till at last, pale and large
I am shipped off by barge,

stripped of pilgrims
by the Byzantian hordes
bringing a new peace by force.
Wishing a new god
they steal my visage.

That's me, God in Man.
Phidias made me,
Phidias the artist,
creator of the creator
who made your religion greater.

You took my icon,
my majesty, my eyes,
my posture, impostor
were it not for the prize –
Man-god's view of God-man.

A rabble sacked me.
I should have known.
There was a woman
with a wide saucer of oil
reflecting light on my face.

Phidias' woman
who had this bright idea
for my Grecian home –
who lit my burning icon
in cold church stone.

Although I was plundered,
in my eternal day
as Phidias' hugely copied gaze
of wonder, hey, I am might
and I still have thunder.

Ode to Grass

Your golf course won't just happen, it is made
by struggling, like poetry, with a vision
trekking through fields, round copses, visualising banks
directing hillocks, utilising slopes
with all your memory and imagination keen,
a knowledge of the country, and of the game.

Your golf hotel needs mortgages and stone;
your clientele require directions,
cajoling, roads, post offices, hot water,
TV reception, grass and brass
and first rate winter and summer accommodation.

It won't just happen any more than a sonnet,
but when it comes, a passionate elegy
or a rollicking ballad – it chooses its own form –
it will seem to have been alive forever,
nor will it look new-made even on its maiden bowl,
when strolling by your partly man-made vale
you watch the antics of its first performers,

and remember with what care you prepared it all,
putting up trees like bureaus, cutting lawns
like carpeting before the baronry
all for a ball and a bit of wood and metal,
passionate madness that will never settle
nor the sensation pass of inspiration,
homage *ode* to grass.

Hare

Jonathan Tulloch

When I was a child my grandfather told me many stories. My favourite ones always concerned the hare.

"Tell me more about the old hare!" I would say, even when it was time for other tales.

Now in my hour of desolation, those stories come back. I hear them as clearly as I did as a child. The guards believe that when I call out I am pleading for mercy. I am not. I am saying: "Grandfather, tell me more about that old hare!"

There are two things to know about the hare. Firstly, though small of stature he is the most cunning of all creation. Secondly, all other animals desire his captivity. Given this state of things, what he lacks in strength and popularity he attempts to make up for with devices of trickery. All the stories illustrate this. For instance, he is able to confuse the elephant who is guarding the waterhole and slake his thirst at leisure, despite the fact that he measures no more than one foot of this immense custodian and a single swat would lay him lifeless on the dust. To get what he needs he must utilise deception. Today and everyday since my incarceration, I have been listening to my grandfather telling me his stories of the hare. If I had not had these to distract me, then how could I have withstood this long nightmare of degredation and pain?

Sometime ago, I cannot tell exactly when as there is no sun or moon here to measure the passage of days and nights, they applied electrodes to my genitals. I have been unable to pass water since that occasion. I am swollen. My urine pools inside, filling my belly like a foul waterhole. I strain for hours, desperate for release but there is not even a trickle, only a terrible dry burning. It is as though I have been dipped into a frothing nest of wasps. Oh! my skin is the earth scorched.

The hare himself would also often come unstuck. Despite his intelligence, he would frequently fall into the hands of his enemies. Then he would have to be double smart to avoid a gruesome fate. I am trying to be double smart too but there seems to be no chance of escape open to me. I do not think I can even walk. I think that they have broken my once powerful legs; shattered my speed. Perhaps I should have forseen all of this when I was that runny nosed child squatting at my grandfather's haunches, listening to his stories as the sun sank from view like a guest who enjoys many evenings of hospitality. For then he asked me what kind of animal I would choose to be and without hesitation I would reply: "Ah! the hare!" At this my grandfather would shrug his shoulders and darkness would pass over his face. Then, I did not know what he knew. I did not realise that to be the hare is to be forever pursued by all the other animals. Only now that I am here , in this hidden hole of the earth, do I understand. Yet perhaps this must be the way. Perhaps a person must choose what he wants to be before he even understands what it means to be this.

As I lie waiting for the next visit from my guards, I have been pondering a mystery. What came first: is it the fantastic cunning of the hare that enrages the other animals so much that they are eager to pin down his ears and maul his slight body, or is it the malicious intentions of his fellow creatures that make his wiles necessary? I contemplate this in the dead silence that surrounds me at all times. I think about it often, like a school child attempting to figure out a difficult task; for to work it out would be to understand so much. Maybe it would be to understand why it is I come to be here in this silent, concrete chamber, acrid with the unpleasant musk of paraffin. I think it would be to understand many other things too.

Not long ago they roped and held me fast like a chicken. Then they beat the soles of my feet until I passed out. I have never known such pain. It shot up into my head. I must have come near to drowning in the agony. For a while I believed myself to be dying. In this torment I remembered the hare. My guards thought I was begging them to stop. I was not. I was really saying: "Grandfather, now I know how it is when they catch the hare!"

I am the hare. And since I am the hare, who are they that delight to beat me? What part do they play in the story?

There are three of them. One is undoubtedly the crocodile. Sometimes they switch a light on to blind my eyes and as its bitter beam arcs the room, showing up the brittle bricks of concrete, I have seen the features of the man who is the crocodile. His eyes are tiny but heavily lidded. His nose is long and appears scaly. He is always wet, foul smelling sweat drips from his body and with every movement droplets fall from him as though he has just emerged from the river. His hands have the strength of jaws as they grip my ankles for his companions to thrash my feet. His aim is to drag me under into his element of physical despair. Then there is the rhinocerous. I dread his bulky shape looming in the corner of the cell. Often he remains at a distance for a long time but just as I take my eyes off him, trusting in the passivity of his presence, he launches himself. Then the horn of his fist gores me and I am tossed high before I fall. As I writhe under his assault he retreats again, but I know to expect him back before too long. The third man is in many ways the worst. I believe him to be that creature, who in the stories is always responsible for the capture of the hare. This man is the tortoise. Not much to fear by the look of him and he certainly lacks the power of his companions. Indeed he is weak and slow. His head is smooth, without a single hair. His body is a shell of fat. His voice, a pitiable whine. Even I could lay him out on the dust of the concrete floor in one swipe and strength is not one of my virtues. Yet he, above the others, is the one to fear. This man is dangerous. The other two huff and puff, unable to disguise their malicious intentions, but he appears gentle and peaceful. He never actually beats me, only watches. Yes, the tortoise is a wily creature. He talks, in the attempt to ensnare me. He lays traps, hoping to secure my neck.

"You can get up and leave here anytime you want," he says. "There is no need for you to suffer. No one else is suffering. Why should you suffer alone?"

As in the stories of my grandfather, he wants the hare to believe that he can outdance the headless chicken. And sometimes I am tempted to listen, for his words are soft, they are the promise of honey to my parched throat; but I know that the only way for the hare to outdance the headless chicken is to chop his own head off. This is the very thing he wishes me to do. He wants to do away with me by my own vanity. This is why he says: "You are too clever to be here in this cell being bruised everyday and night. You see that there is a way out. You are an intelligent man. Surely you can see the way out? Is this really where you want your education to lead you?"

It is the names of my comrades that he wants. His desire is for me to supply their names and addresses. He wants a list of all the other hares. Only I am double smart and realise that if I were to tell him, he would kill me immediately. Soon he will kill me anyway, so what have I to gain by betrayal? I think he already sees that I will not tell him. In our country hares have had to learn a new trick. We have learnt to be brave when we are unable to escape our pursuers, for if we are not then they will hunt out all our kind and they will kill them, one by one. Also we have come to learn that sometimes, there are things more important than mere survival of life. This is one of those times.

This morning, or was it tonight? (Oh sun and moon, you have both been banished from this world of burning pain and sorrows that evaporate on the concrete floor!) the tortoise spoke to me. He whined and lisped painfully. I did not answer him, so he stepped back to let the crocodile through. The crocodile slid towards me and sliced off my ear. Then he placed the ear in my mouth and made me chew, all the while the tortoise looked at me, as though he was full of sympathising. Soon the other will be cut off. Perhaps I will slowly be made to consume myself. It doesn't matter. Even if you cut off his handsome pair of ears, you cannot stop a hare from being a hare. As I ate, I puzzled over something. In all the stories my grandfather told me, the hare was a lazy creature, living off the work of other animals without turning a hand himself. This is why they wanted to capture him. This is why the guards say they want to capture me and my comrades. They call us leeches, enemies of the state; because of this they think we are dangerous, vermin to be extinguished. But we are not. The hare is not wilfully lazy. This is to misrepresent him. The reason he does not aid the others in their enterprises is because he is clever. He sees what is really going on. Really he wants the world to be different. The crocodile, the rhino and the tortoise consider the world to be fine as it is. Together they control it. This is why there is conflict. This is why I am dying in this dark pit, unbefriended by the frank light of sun and moon.

I am the hare. Listen to me carefully. For the first time you are hearing the hare tell his own story and it is a story that the young must hear rather than the old tales. Grandfather, I am not angry that you did not understand the way things truly are. You came before, at a time when the people had not yet learned to be rigorous with the truth of the world. I did not choose to be the hare because I am lazy or coveted a life without work. I have not sat and watched the other animals spending days digging the waterhole and then sauntered down to trick my share. The hare is cunning for different reasons than indolence.

There is a sound at the door. Even without ears my keen hearing is not impaired. A key tinkles in the lock. That is the music I fear. The door opens like a mouth. The guards are here. They show themselves on the threshold. Something is different. I think there is something different about how they are standing at the door. I have waited for this moment a long time. If he knows that death must come, which animal, hunted or hunter, wishes to prolong his agony? The tortoise comes towards me first. It must be that way. His step is slow and awkward, a shuffle. In his hand is a gun. Such is his finesse! It would be too easy to simply batter my brains into a pile of dung steaming on the grassless concrete floor, but even to the end, the tortoise knows better. He is an expert in terror. For the first time I am truly frightened. The gun points at me like an evil finger. This is how it should be. He knows that this is his final chance to get from me what he wants. The final torture. A charge from the rhino or a lunge from the crocodile, and I could ride the blows, hoping it was just another severe beating. I could believe that until my head rings with the silence of death. I could to the last. With a gun, however, there can be no mistake, no room for pretence. I am staring at my death. It is a coiled snake of immaculate venom. I do not care. Put it to my throat. Let me feel its hiss in my bleeding eardrums. I will defeat even the cold knowledge of my extinction because to do so is to play the ultimate trick on my enemies. Soon I will have won. The moment he pulls that trigger I emerge the victor. The hare will win and one day the victory will be apparent, even to you grandfather. My guards believe that I am pleading for my life. I am not. What I am truly saying is: "Grandfather, let there be more of that old hare! Let the ancestors encourage our children to choose to be this small but determined animal. Make their hearts cunning and their cunning brave. For they will need it when they realise the truth of the world. For the poor will always be chased and forever sought for capture and enslavement. What we lack in strength and popularity, give us through cunning!"

In a moment my body will be slumped on the ground and they will think that the legs kick out because of nerves. It will not be due to this. They will kick out because at last they they are walking free and are happy to celebrate their freedom. The crocodile, the rhinocerous and the tortoise have failed to understand that you cannot destroy the hare by killing one of them. You cannot stifle the nature of a people by killing them. First you must steal their nature and this is not something you can easily take. Oh my oppressor, oh the oppressors of my people, you of the crocodile and rhino hide, you of tortoise deception, do you not understand? Do you not know that for each hare you cull, another two are born with strong legs, fine ears and hearts that are ready for the ample discovery of freedom?

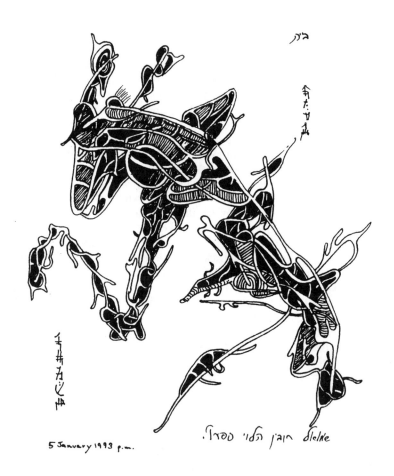

בין

5 January 1993 p.m.

Illustration by Robin Spark

W S Milne

Paradise 2

Ay you! close-heelan in pinnaces,
whase pilot's sang, ship straucht and true,
course chairted, the ship choruses –
ti shore turn back, ye've time ti rue!
The bothome's deep, sae dinnae try it;
mind me, yersels, if hame ye loe!
Sea-roads nae kent, ma craft then tackit,
Minerva win-backed, Apollo oor steersman,
Muses oor guides, ti the Bears pyntit.
But nae, och nae, fine sauls wha heivin
afore aftimes have raxed uptill!
Whase breid ablow ti us ye've gien
– nae fear frae you, trust ma keel,–
on furr and rig-heid, on aa the swaws,
ahin ma yawl you'll pu livil –
like them, fine-stoundit, the heroes
at Colchis, sa michtie Jason steer the pleuch,
the mair will be your mazement, readers.
Can niver dee, thon pairt, ti the warld wi us
did come, thrist for heivin niver slakit–
skelpt us on, like scuddan cluds
at a fair lick, fast, – gazit,
ye'll see, on Heivin Beatrice, and on her, me: –
straucht and fair, richt on tairget
mesel I foond, richt mazit:
A ferlie ma sicht fair stonisht,
aye, a mervel! She pirled aroond
– keekin ma mind, its feeling, thochts –
blithe she was, and bonnie, lownd:
"Heize yersel ti God," she said, "Your sinse
be thankrife, wha wi the ferst ster maks us soond."
And straucht awa, oor mense,
it seemit, was cludit, but cleir-like seen,
as whan the sun a luminescence
maks, spirks aff a diamant's sheen –
likewise wi us, eternitie's jynted
(square-like) as watter a beam o licht, suin,
taks, but in itsel is niver changit:
bides for aye juist like itsel, ken –
twa bodies fine thegither bidit –
me and her: hou monie mair, eager, eident,
His mergh has kennit?
In whase hoosehauld oor being's ardent?
His and oors? Whit faith hadds here is nae cleir brookan,
mind, ower thar itsel is findit.
Whit's cleir is truth, it's nae for dressan,

mair and mair oor langing's parchit (here's me spickan!)
"Leddie dear, it's Him I'm thankan,
clear, devotit, frae the warld hurtlan
mortals, aye; taks us up, tapsietourie,
aa else followan,
thae body-bands, thae stobs are sair, whit are thai?
Eh? aa fair mirkie! Like ti branks,
Cain's tale dae tell, dae thai, ti them ablouw?"
She smirkled. "Na, nae nearer – sunks!
thon curtain sinse can niver rent, mind how! –
thouch fowk hae speired, and gowkit, aa ranks.
The wey reason prised, heichts are here ti shouw.
Wonder's shaifts micht mair be bricht!
Aye, and you, come nou, yersel, bestouw,
whit is it? Spick!" "It's mair the licht,
sheens lesser thar, and here the mair? A miracle?"
"Na! Na! Och losh!" she siched,
"In error's sunks you are, your thochts are shauchled!
But here me nou. I'll see ye richt!
Fu monie the lichts (they're nae aa bauchled)
the echth spheir glints,
apperances, aye, they're aa aff-kilter, aff-beam, crock.
Nou listen here, there is a difference,
sure, it's nae one vertue bands the lot!
Nae wey how! Thouch reason saiys, it seems,
some are fine, and some are yowk. They're awfa pyot!
Graces vary, princeps differ (aa bar ain)
mind yow; reasoning alwayis likes things richt!
And how! If scarcitie it were alane
gart blebs ti tash,
the heids would be (ye see it plain?)
aa turnit gash!
– aa throuch bare, at aince, like leaves atween
the quair's pages, a folio amassit,
or maet compressit, fat and lean.
It canna be! Naewey! Else
the sun's eclipsit, passit, his raiys would leam
throuch and throuch the stuff that's strippit –
(nae the case ava, it's juist nae claimit) –
like picturs throuch a keeking-gless slew,
throuch and throuch we'd wach it,
richt? skites aff its leids, true,
frae further back, ye'd say –
caists, projecks, and derker clews
the image: a cantrip, aye,
juist, if ye've the nerve ti try it.
Science the spring-heid is, by!
Experiment the profite.
Set oot twa glesses
distant, a thrid in sicht,
atween the twa that faces –

ahin your heid a licht:
they'll caist the mair, wi graces
sure, back, a glorie bricht:
for the flamb reflecks
that's far awa, the same, the micht
that's mingled fine, protecks,
like snaw, the grun, 'til bare
the thaw begins ti melt:
pits by the cauldrife fite and sair,
'til the yirth is strippit clean,
naturalitie delate, as whan a duncan ster
delichts us aa, prinks the living een.
And this it is, hou far!
God's peace and quiet is athin,
His Heivin gloryan,
anither heivin,
wi flambeaux lit, varyand,
is, the spheirs, the-niver-ti-be-repeated ain,
bi aa weys jilpan:
the tide aye bidan,
the ebb and flouw o life careeran,
the differences the warld bestrides:
and sae it is there is nae followan.
Frae rank ti rank each shoves the ither, bridegroom, bride,
ain on anither alwayis bearing –
wach the wey it is I ride,
ye'll suin be hurryan,
suin ye'll ken the truth, a fack,
side bi side wi me be bidan,
the maisured road, the halie walk
it is the maister finds:
the truth the metal traisures
wi his haimmer draws, heivin's mind,
manifold fires wheel and gyre
athin oor stour the saul that hides
throuch and throuch your liths,
your beuchs, the flamb that slides, moolds and clims:
likewise sters
flouw, divide –
a multitiude o difference
aye, in unitie abide.
Owreairching brilliance,
Intelligence grouws, in guidness staiys.
Whit sentience! vertue scintills,
bodies find
aathing spirkles,
oor een, oor life, oor minds!
Naitur glaiks, and aawey prinkles,
this wey aa things tend –
derkness, brichtness,
aa things boonded, penned."

William Neill

The New Charitie

Nou guid-will is abreid, ma freens, ye see
hou ilka pauper-bodie is a laird,
that no lang syne wes jist an idle caird
thay'd pit in jyle an caa awa the key.

Nou thare's mair hairt, an mair o charitie
nae langer jam the morn, but jam the day –
but dinna fash, ye need puir fowks ti say
hou nobil is thair generositie!

For athoot beggars an the honest puir
hou micht fowk shaw belief in Jesus Christ,
the charitie o Christians an thair feres?

Say: "Be as kindlie nou as aye ye wir,"
yon's hou ti pit thair purses ti the test,
hou can thay gie thair awms gin naebodie speirs?

caird: a vagrant
caa awa: throw away
fash: worry
feres: companions
awms: alms
speirs: asks

(In 1847 the govenor o Rome made provision for 200 beggars)
(*Le limosine demonetate* by G G Belli, owerset frae Romanesco)

The Gentrie's Marrow

Och, daena speik ti me aboot yon baund
me that's alang wi thaim the haill year roun!
I ken the gentrie lik I ken ma haund
an hes the feck o thaim ablo ma thoom.

I ken ilk hoorshop whaur they're ti be fund
I ken thair debts wi ilka shark in toun,
I ken the lees thay skail aboot the laund,
the traps thay set ti caa an unfreen doun.

But lat me say that ilka singil day,
I'm wi the duke and hae ma honour haill
an ilka gait he gangs, thare I's be taen.

An gin thay're et high jinks then I'm thare tae:
ye'll fairlie see hou I enjoy masel
dinin wi thaim, or daein whit thay're daein.

feck: majority
unfeen: rival
ilk, ilka: each
gin: if
high jinks: horseplay

(*Er cammerata de li siggnori* by G G Belli,
owerset frae Romanesco)

The Dochter's Fee

The Gala nicht he stairtit the affair
he saa her, fancied her an gied a wink;
syne saa her ti the dure an whit d'ye think?
He fleetched wi her ti tak him up the stair.

Withoot as much as speirin ma permeesion
he cam in ben the hoose wi her at heel;
eftir thrie days she kent she wesna weill.
An syne ye'll ken the cause o yon condeition.

Eftir thrie months o threipin, whit d'ye think?
thon lairdling senns thrie geinies for the deed.
I shudna taen the siller, dae ye say?

Had he no been o sich guid faimily
He wadna hae gat aff withoot a stink –
thrie geinies for the puir quine's maidenhead.

fleetch: coax
geinies: guineas
threipin: insistence

(*El fatto de la fijja* by G G Belli,
owerset frae Romanesco)

The Attack

Trevor Edmands

Lois put down her gun and went to pick some flowers. She had meant to do this for some time but she had been putting it off for some reason that she could no longer remember. It is strange, she thought, how excitement makes one forget the simplest things.

The flowers were to have been a thank you token for one of her friends. In fact, they were to have been a thank you token for the gun she had just put down. This too she had forgotten, temporarily at least.

She felt at peace – it was a lovely day for flower arranging and that was what she was doing. Lois felt good, in fact very good, in fact she could not remember feeling better in her entire life.

Lois had had the gun for several weeks and had felt that she ought to have contacted her friend a lot earlier to explain why she had not returned it sooner, and of course to tell her how things were going with her generally, but somehow Frank had always intervened.

In fact Frank was the reason she had borrowed the gun in the first place. But then he had always had a way of thwarting all her plans. At that he was, she thought, almost a genius. He managed this, it seemed to her, by timing his needs so scrupulously that whenever she had just reached a stage of personal freedom with enough space and leisure to consider her own life and what she might have wanted to do for herself, he would appear. He would, as it were, come round the corner holding his head in both hands and screwing up his eyes so that he could hardly see for himself and demand that she get him the tablets.

It wasn't always like this of course, sometimes Frank would appear at such moments with a bat for her to play ball with him, or with one of his sexy grins – one of his "let's go frolic, doll" grins which made Lois feel like a big overgrown doll for hours afterwards.

However Lois was not the complaining type. She, as Frank had so often pointed out, both publicly and privately, was the one who had made all the play for him originally, and he had been a good sport about it all and had allowed her to be around and attend him. "And his needs" she would have liked to have added on more than one occasion, but she never did – she always simply smiled. She kept her thoughts to herself, always had.

Frank's mother had always insisted that Frank was too sensitive and too delicate for her to ever be capable of adequately ministering to his needs. She had a way of implying that Lois was somehow too 'brassy' and was a fundamentally crude person who, no matter how hard she tried, would never be capable of any sort of refinement or sensitivity.

Lois did not like Frank's mother but she was too afraid of her to let it show. Today however, was different. Today, for the first time since she had known her, she felt completely at ease and fully confident about her own competence. She had no fear whatever of either Frank or his dismal mother. Today, for the first time, she felt as though Frank's mother was at the bottom of the drive staring over the fence at her as she gathered the flowers. She could 'feel' that disapproving stare but it no longer mattered. She felt as though this was rather like a very realistic dream in which her mother in law was looking more and more disapproving until her face was becoming so distorted that it had to be painful to the facial muscles, whilst she, Lois, was radiant and utterly serene before her.

There seemed no need for Lois to express her feelings towards Frank's mother other than in the way she was doing already, by being totally absorbed in arranging the flowers and in smelling their fragrance.

On the bed lay Frank, dead. Lois looked at him and smiled for a moment before she resumed arranging the flowers in a vase. Somehow this very act which Frank had scorned as "a typically vacuous, typically female pursuit", made Lois feel happy, at peace, and above all, 'free'.

"I'll ring her and tell her soon", she said to herself aloud. She looked at Frank again and smiled once more.

One of Frank's most amusing characteristics, which had played some part at least in his death, was his utter self absorption which had until just now, always enabled him to get his own needs met. It simply did not occur to him that the gratification of others might not be inextricably linked with his own. Consequently he was especially proud of himself as a lover. In his lovemaking he was ecstatic. Lois did not share Frank's ecstasies; except as a spectator.

On what Lois had thought was going to be their honeymoon, Lois had closed her eyes and waited to be absorbed in some beautiful union. When this did not happen – indeed, when Frank first said, "Let me have it, hon" at the moment of ejaculation, her eyes popped open, and she saw that Frank's eyes were tight closed during his final thrusts.

That 'hon' was the closest Frank ever came to expressing affection towards her. But for that 'hon' she thought she need never have been there at all, and probably wasn't so far as Frank was concerned.

For quite some time now Lois had had her eyes open during the whole dreadful mismatch and saw that from the time he entered her to the "let me have it, hon" he had his eyes tightly closed. He was blind. He didn't want to see her. He was probably fantasising that she was someone else.

Lois would have liked to explain Frank's death to his mother but she knew that she would never be able to tell anyone. "Some things are too private", her mother in law would often say. Usually this preceded an attempt to pry into some intimacy.

"Some things are private", she mused as she took the flowers to the window table." "Some things are too intimate to discuss with anyone". She smiled. She felt serene.

Her mind went over Frank's final ecstatic union with her and she thought how this had also been ecstatic for her – orgasmic almost. As Frank reared back, eyes tight shut, Lois took the gun from under her pillow. She held it in front of her face and aimed it at Frank's nose.

"Let me have it", he said, omitting for once the "hon".

"Did he sense something outside himself at death?", she wondered aloud.

Certainly his eyes opened a little ahead of schedule. Equally certainly they opened wider than usual . . . and his mouth also. Louis didn't have to squeeze the trigger. Of course the gun wasn't loaded in any case.

Frank's ecstasy moved too quickly from the pelvic pump to the bloodpump . . . and a little more jerking and he lay quite still.

Now Lois looked at him and sighed. She felt that she had satisfied them both at last. They had each attained a kind of peace.

Just beyond him were the flowers with the sunlight streaming through their petals on the window table. Next to these was the telephone.

*art*WORK

The North's Independent Arts Newspaper

*art*WORK is available throughout Scotland and into the North in arts centres, galleries, museums and theatres. It's available on free distribution because that way we can reach a sizeable audience, but it's certainly not free to produce, so we very much welcome the support of subscribers to bolster our much prized independence. Fill in and send off the form below and we'll do the rest.

*PLEASE SEND MY REGULAR COPY OF *art*WORK TO THIS ADDRESS*

Name: ....

Address: ....

....

I ENCLOSE   *£5.00 (6 issues)*   ❏   *£10.00 (12 issues)*   ❏

Send (with cheque/PO) to: Famedram Publishers Ltd, PO Box No 3, Ellon, AB41 9EA

"TI SEND US JOY THAT LESTS AYE"

Lallans is published by The Scots Language Society and gives priority to new quality creative writing in Scots. An annual subscription includes three issues of *Lallans* (February, May and November) and costs £10 (£12 outwith Europe).

The Scots Language Society
The A. K. Bell Library
York Place, Perth PH2 8AP

THE MAGAZINE FOR WRITING IN SCOTS

Rody Gorman

Sgiobaltachd

'S ionann taigh sgiobalta
'S inntinn sgiobalta, canar –
Cha ghèill mi dha
Idir idir idir:

Tha m'inntinn fhèin
Làn de threallaich

A' stobadh a-mach air feadh an àite
No am falach ann an cùiltean
'S cus rudan aosda 's briste
A chaidh bho fheum bho shean
Ach a tha mi air a shon sin
Leisg a shadail air falbh.

Tidiness

A tidy house
Is a tidy mind, they say –
I'll have none of it
at all

My own mind
Is full of junk

Sticking out all over the place
Or hidden in crannies
And too many old and broken things
Which lived out their usefulness long ago
But which, in spite of all that,
I'm reluctant to throw away.

Cidsin

Chaidh an cidsin againn sgioblachadh
'S às dèidh dha bhith air a dhèanamh

Agus treallaich na laighe
Air feadh an àite

Thuirt thusa gun robh doras a bharrachd ann
'S thuirt mise gun robh preas eile dhìth oirnn.

Kitchen

Our kitchen was done up
And after the job was complete

And all sorts of rubbish
Scattered about the place

You said that there was an extra door
And I said we were missing a cupboard.

Anns A' Phoca

Chuir mi romham gun cosgainn
Mìosan an t-samhraidh
Shuas anns a'Chuilthionn
Far an d'rachamaid an-uiridh

Ach an cuirinn a h-uile gin dhiubh
Air ais anns a' phoca
A dh'fhàg thu fhèin falamh
Nuair a gh'fhalbh thu an-dràsda.

In The Bag

I decided that I'd spend
The summer months
Up in the Cuilinn
Where we used to go last year

So that I could put every one of them
Back in the bag
Which you left empty
When you left just now.

A'Ghaidlig

Chì mi bhuam thu gu soilleir:
'S e bh' annad riamh ach a' Ghàidhlig
A thog m' inntinn cho mòr
Ach nach robh riamh agam air mo theangaidh
'S i a' caochladh
Nam fhianais beag is beag.

Gaelic

I see you clearly:
All you ever were was the Gaelic language
Which elevated my spirit so much
But which I never had off pat
And which is decaying
In front my eyes.

Uidheam-Stiuridh

Chunnaic mi do charbad
'S gun thu fhèin na bhroinn

'S shaoil mi mar mhiastadh
Gun cuirinn às dhan uidheam-stiùiridh,

Chan ann gus do chur far an rathaid,
Dìreach gus do chur air ais thugam fhìn.

Steering Mechanism

I saw your car
Without you in it

And I thought, out of mischief,
That I'd bugger up the steering mechanism,

Not to put you off the road,
Just to make you come back to me.

Siaban

Tha mi glacte aig na siabain
Ris an seall mi leam fhìn air an oidhche,
Chan ann airson de lèirsinn
A bheir iad air cùisean a' chridhe,
Dìreach san dòchas
Gun glan iad mo chuimhn' ort às.

Soap

I'm hooked on soaps
Which I watch on my own at night,
Not for the vision they bring
Regarding matters of the heart,
Just in the hope
That they'll wipe away my memory of you.

Stones

Eva Fleg Lambert

It was an unusually hot day. She stooped to pick up a stone and throw it on the wall behind her and thought, vaguely, *it is as if* . . . And she straightened and could not finish her thought. In her mind there remained a vague uneasiness of experiences past, experiences taken but not understood, the wisdom of hindsight (even) raked clean from her mind like the stones from her garden, leaving the earth smooth, ready for the fresh seeds which she still had to buy at the local hardware shop. She smiled to herself as she pulled the rake through the velvety dark soil of her garden, in her mind seeing the seeds sprouting in neat rows to grow into pleasantly nodding blooms. And then her brow ruckled as she stooped to pick up another stone and cast it from her garden. It was, again, *as if* . . .

She closed her eyes, the sun red through her eyelids, and, with forehead still ruckled, concentrated, gathering the vague threads of thought into some coherence. *As if* . . . oh yes, she could finish her thought if she really wanted, for, she knew: *it was as if her past might creep up on her.* But she mustn't brood, she told herself sternly as she bent to her rake once more. She must rid her head of the past, the way she was ridding her garden of stones so that her new life could take root. Yes.

She was here now, she told herself firmly as she prodded a rather large stone, here on this remote tip of a remote island of a remote spit of Northern mainland on a piece of land which she could fashion herself into a garden of *her* design, which she pictured like a tea cosy around the low whitewashed cottage which was almost, but not quite, as she wanted it. She still had to get Iain to come up from the village and replace those plastic drainpipes which he had installed after she quite implicitly told him she wanted nothing plastic in or on her house. He had insisted that metal ones were unattainable but she had pointed to a derelict cottage with metal drains leaning at precarious and useless angles and Iain had nodded, "Aye." However, when she returned from England, bringing her last carload of belongings thus firmly closing that chapter of her life, she had found the plastic drains in place. And the roof patched with reddish Welsh slates and not the Balachulish which she had wanted.

She was down on her hands and knees now, trying to budge the stone but it was even larger than she had thought. She went and got the garden fork and tried to prod it out but it remained firmly in place.

"Gettin' ready to plant the tatties?" Neil, a man in his seventies who lived with his sister down the road, had limped silently up behind her. She gave a startled cry, like a bird ready to take flight. "Didn't mean to frighten you," he apologised.

She quickly regained her composure and smiled at him. "Actually, I'm trying to dislodge this stone. It's rather larger than I thought."

"Aye, it'll be going down to Australia more like."

"Oh you are silly, Neil," she pronounced his name to rhyme with eel, drawing out the e's which made the poor man squirm. She was poised like a bird eyeing a worm. "I think I'm going to need a pick. Could I borrow one from you?"

"That you could."

"Thank you."

"If I had one but, oh no," and he shook his head from side to side, "I can't say I've got one to lend you."

She was not sure whether he meant he had one, but didn't want to lend it to her, or that he didn't have one at all. She tried not to show her annoyance in any case. Instead, she smiled brightly at him, tilting her head to one side. "I'm going to plant flowers here, Neil. Flowers to brighten the land and sweeten the air." She smiled once more, benignly she thought, and thinking thus she stretched the smile causing a red spot to appear on each cheek.

"If the wind doesn't do for 'em."

She straightened her back, bringing her chin up. "I've thought of that Neil," she said, not to be outdone. "I've planted a row of Scots pines as windbreak." Neil didn't say anything, merely nodded. "But now I've got to get this stone out."

"You could plant around it," he said, "or maybe make one of those rock gardens." He tapped the stone with his stick. "a rock garden."

"But I'm having a rockery," she pronounced the word carefully, give it its full three syllables, "Over there, by the side of the house."

"Wind'll get it for sure there," Neil said shaking his head. She closed her eyes and sighed loudly. "Well, best be goin'." He turned and limped away.

"The plants in the rockery are low growing," she called after him, not wanting to be outdone. "Besides, the rocks will protect them." He waved his stick in the air in reply, but didn't turn. *Silly old man,* she thought as she hit the stone with her rake.

Tall and thin, a woman in her mid-forties who had appeared one summer striding down the road with a pack on her back, the locals took no more notice of her than any other visitor to the island. But when she returned the following summer, this time in an old 2CV, nosing about the uninhabited croft that was strung out along the cliff like a tattered patchwork quilt, eyebrows were raised, lace curtains fluttered and lilted speculations wove through the baaing of sheep during the shearing. The croft had belonged to old Hector and there were a few in the community who wanted possession. When the Commission, in its wisdom, allocated the croft and house to the tall thin English woman, the speculations turned to muttering and old grievances wept like suppurating wounds. But to the tall thin English woman, there were only polite smiles and an unspoken distance adhered to on both sides.

She continued to rake, casting the stone from the smoothed soil, but the large stone remained. *I'll get Iain to remove it for me,* she thought. *And then when the house is finished, the trees grown and the garden is blooming, with the fences mended, then I'll stock the land.* She was going to breed sheep, sheep for wool which she would spin into yarn, dye herself with only local dyeplants, and sell to tourists at first, but, she was sure, her product would catch on and she'd be selling on the mainland, even in England. A friend had drawn up the plan for her which she had submitted to the Crofters' Commission when she had applied for possession of the croft and house. The locals might think her mad and incompetent but she'd show them, oh yes. This was not going to be some hair-brained scheme, no, not like . . . She refused to think of it.

Which wasn't possible, of course. The more she insisted on *not* thinking of it, the more she thought of it so that it dominated her life. "No," she said aloud, "This will be different." She looked round in alarm, fearful someone had heard her and think she was losing her mind. A single gull cried above, then wheeled in a swoop out over the sea.

In the evening, a slight breeze frilling flowery curtains, the open window framing a shimmering silver sea, she sat, one hand on cheek, while with her other she fingered the corner of an unopened letter which fluttered, like the curtains, in her lap. She had recognised the handwriting of course. It was from him. *Him. Probably an apology of sorts. He wanted her to take him back?* She humphed to herself and got up, crumpling the letter in her hand. *No. That part of her life was over.* She threw the letter into the fireplace, then realized there was, of course, no fire so picked it up and set a match to it, holding it under the chimney so the smoke would drift upwards, then dropped the still burning letter, and watched as the ashes lifted and did a feint twisting dance from the breeze.

She returned to sit by the window, staring out towards horizons distant as unseen stars.

Exactly one year ago, they, he and she, had planned on opening a vegetarian café in the Devonshire village in which they had, separately, arrived only two month previously: she from a year's travelling in Australia, he from teaching English in Barcelona. An odd combination, the intellectual and the craftswoman – not that he would ever have labelled himself thus; she was honest enough to acknowledge at least that much. But he had woo'd her – and the term was not too old-fashioned to describe their courtship – with poetry and long silences while she had responded by spinning yarn from fence torn fleece and then knitting him a warm woolly hat. It was high summer.

By the time autumn had arrived she was cooking him meals which they ate before a log fire. When the first wintry blasts rattled the window frames of her rented cottage he had suggested, in rhyming couplets, that they live together. She had, with a charming tilt of her head, agreed, assuming he would move in with her for, after all, she had made the cottage although only rented, into such a snug little nest. His cottage on the other hand, stuck in a cleft of hill overlooking Dartmoor, was exposed to the weather on all sides and badly needed rendering. "But I own. Why pay rent?"

And then she had the idea of opening a vegetarian cafe. In his cottage. She was sure they'd get planning permission and if they got started right

Illustration by Alfons Bytautas

away, it could possibly be ready for the summer season. They'd have an income. Stability.

He was uncertain.

She was not.

She was strong willed, insistent, but with a quiet-voiced demure manner and thus it was that he moved into her cottage. She applied for and received planning permission and the building work on the conversion of his cottage into a restaurant began. He made arrangements for the builders to come, but it was she who supervised them, while he watched his bank balance dwindle. He wrote articles for the local paper, became a relief English teacher at the college but still his money disappeared along with his patience. He had not written a single poem since he had moved in with her.

While she, on the other hand, had gained some weight and importance in her own mind as she ordered builders about, insisting on oak here, pitch pine there and quarry tiles on the floor. When he walked out of her cottage into his almost re-modelled one taking with him one of his young male students, she was more outraged than hurt. Abandoning all plans as quickly as she had instigated them, she decided to head north where, presumably, the air would be clearer and life more predictable.

The days shortened, her flowers bloomed then bowed their heads to winds freshening from the West. She closed her windows, tucked the curtains to keep out the drafts and lit her fire. Snugly smug she baked her bread, cooked her meals, spun a fleece given to her by Neil. She had no fear of the elements.

In that remote corner of that remote island the first gales came early that year, taking with them as they sped across to the Mainland a number of tiny Scots pine trees, some slate roof tiles and one section of old metal drainpipe. But no stones, not a one.

Colin Mackay

Poem at Christmas (Then)

Then I loved the frost,
the cry of the white winter
approaching from the hills,
and the breath that walked beside us
when it was conker-time
and we went rummaging among
the chestnut trees on London Road.

In the morning
boys delivered rolls and papers,
and milk froze in
its bottles on the doorstep,
and coins were cold to touch.

It made even school
almost bearable,
it made the air sting
our knees red,
froze the smoke to the chimneys,
and the hills were snowed-in
at the street's end
where they rose like a vision
of another world.

And the Co-op carthorse
came plodding up Leith Walk
with his shoes clinking
on the tram-lines,
leaving heaps of golden dung
that we scrambled out with shovels
to collect, still steaming,
for our mothers' window boxes.

Then night came walking in
over the roofs,
and the police constable
who paced past our door
with a Lantern
drew his cape close.

And I heard his booted feet
acquire a new sound,
a muffled, crunching sound,
and I rushed to my window
to see him pass,
a steady black figure
arm-in-arm with his frozen breath
crossing the quiet snow.

Poem at Christmas (Now)

Now there is no snow,
only the rain that comes with cat-like sounds
and sets the aerials trembling
in the cold red light
as I squelch home from work,
avoiding the freezing puddles
and fallen chestnuts on London Road.

Avoiding also (or trying to)
the trap of regretting a past
that never was, I still wonder
whether the blackbird's song
is not shorter, like the days,

the hill smaller,
and the world a less exciting place.
Yet the air speaks kindness,
the smoke is gone,
and I am no longer terrified
of the teacher's tawse
and the playground bully
who made me weep with pain and humiliation.
Be thankful for that, at least.

In the evening rush-hour
the traffic pours over Leith Walk
where I used to play
my childhood games,
taking us home to television,
dinner in the micro-wave
and the computer bleeping
in the children's room.

Home is where I assemble my silences
and listen for the bells of winter
that no one else seems to hear
ringing out over the roofs
where phantoms go
in the slithering rain.

Here on the ladder of time
I climb the darkness:
days of the past
with its heart full of snow,
nights of the past
interlocked with longing,
years – oh, years when
I loved the frost!

Sutherland

It is the third night I have heard it,
the cart my grandfather drove
south from Sutherland which they called
"the land of the Mackays"
in the year Queen Victoria died.
I turn over in bed at the century's end
and awaken, bemused,
on a wind-swept hillside,
and I see the cart pass below on the white road
behind a slow-moving horse,
and there is a man I have never seen,
Uilleam Ban, with his young wife
sitting high on a mound of furniture,
and in her arms –
   and I look into the eyes
of the child who is in her arms
and I see my father
before his hair grew grey and his eyes sad
with disappointment, depression and death.
I see him as he was
when the world was full of wonder
and tomorrow was a distant cry
rising over the hills.
And suddenly my heart fills with love
for this thrawn old man who is now gone,
whom I will never see again in this world,
from whose lips I will never hear
the praise I longed for, nor exchange
the greetings of those who come home
   the twilight.

Tonight the white sheep of Sutherland congregate
about the ruined dwellings of a vanished people,
and I wonder what endures in this
desolate place, what can endure?
The darkness is lit with bright eyes
that are not our eyes, they are not
the eyes of Angus Dubh and Clan Aoidh,
not the valiant ones of Reay and Strathnaver
whom my father often told me about,
marching proudly beside his cart in that year
their croft was abandoned to the winds.
They were the last of the peasants,
Uilleam Ban and his family,
and I, their pale descendant,
am dying of forgetfulness.
Too late I learned to love their ways,

and now that fire is cold,
blow and blow on it as I will.
And though the love between us was fine,
enduring as the castle on its rock,
beautiful as all the flowers of Edinburgh,
I know now, this night,
in the city ruffled with east wind,
by the Forth leaping under its bridges,
that those stones of Sutherland
shall lie tumbled in their far green pastures
until the sun goes down on human sorrow.

Granton Shore

It is hard to think that the sun
setting over Bosnia tonight
has set on you forever,
and you will not be there
to greet its rising on the Drina,
nor Ahmad, nor young Ludmilla,
nor any of your people.
It is hard to think it.

And though tonight I walk
along the Granton shore
and see the glow of distant Mossmoran
and the coastal lights of Fife
pricking the darkness like gunfire,
there is no satisfaction in my heart
when I think of the aid we brought,
the food, the medicine, the absence of guns.
I wish I had been your soldier.
I wish I had been there to meet
those killers with a gun in my hand.
I wish I had killed for you,
I wish I had died for you
Svetlana
that you might have lived
with Ahmad and young Ludmilla
and all your people
to see the sun rise again
and again because it is
oh, so good!

And though the last vile belch of communism
be no more than a bad memory,
and though the butcher of Belgrade
is being driven from his lair,
I cannot rejoice tonight
as I would wish,
because my heart is with a massacred village,
and I see again the four-and-forty people
we found in that red field,
the four-and-forty we shovelled under the weeping earth.
And I cannot be reconciled
to the fact that the men who did it
are sitting at home tonight watching television
and making love to their wives,
the men who raped you
so brutally,
so many times,
then cut your fair throat.

Memories

Ancient voice,
to hear you is to remember the earth
after rain, scented with decay
and rich in golden dung.

Once in a knot of time I lifted
the lid off a cowpat with a stick
and uncovered swarms of yellow horseflies
that rose humming drowsily
in a blur of silver wings.

Then the country bus went barking up the road
leaving blue cones of exhaust stretched
across the middle of the afternoon,
and the midge-ridden bracken was jungle-high,
and the trees reached all the way to heaven.

Ancient voice,
to hear you is to remember the sky
curtained with clouds
white as seagulls.

That was childhood, sepia,
a row of forgotten aunts in the frame,
and behind them – Spitfires,
their sharp noses uplifted
and shimmering in the sun.

Young men in airforce blue surrounded us
laughing, they ruffled my short hair,
their own cropped, shiny with brylcreem.
I sat in the cockpit,
a wall of dials faced me.
"On your tail, Scottie!" –
the air was thick with bullets.

Ancient voice,
to hear you is also to remember the firth
and the cry of the flood-tide
reaching to its end.

A raw-kneed boy stands on the quay
and the waves come seeking him with planks,
with bottles, torn netting, seaweed
and the foam of passing merchantmen
who wear their red ensigns gloriously
like crowns.

At day's close the dark tenements
dance along the shore,
their black roofs fly off
towards the evening glow,
and on the horizon Fife sparkles with green light.
Then the fishwife comes down
over the stones with her dripping creel,
winks at me as she fills her pipe,
and coughs a stream of gluey phlegm
into the churning salt.

Once in a knot of time
I was those things.
Now when I hear you,
the day falls open,
and night rushes in with its memories
of a happy land
where no one ever wept.

Southfields 1 edited by Raymond Friel and Richard Price. A new big little magazine. New poetry by John Burnside, Robin Fulton, Elizabeth James, David Kinloch, Edwin Morgan, Tom Paulin, and many others. Essays on Paulin and Muldoon; New Poetries; Scottish Fiction in the 1930s; the art of Joseph Davie; Black Film since the 1960s; What was Wrong with the New Poetry Generation; John Burnside; Kathleen Jamie; Racism and the TUC; and more. Illustrated by Edwin Morgan's photocopioids. £4.00. 180pp. For an extra £1.00 EM's *Colour Supplement* (only available here) will be included. *Southfields 2: Exiles and Emigrés* edited by Raymond Friel, David Kinloch and Richard Price. Living in some other place?... Read this. New poems by James Berry, D. M . Black, Christina Dunhill, Robin Fulton, John Greening, Penelope Shuttle and many more. Fiction by James Cressey and Val Warner. Translations from the Danish of Henrik Nordbrandt and the German of Stella Rotenberg. Victor Serge in the Earthquake Zone (trans John Manson), Peter Manson in Fractal-Land, A Short Film About Ring-Pulls... Alasdair Gray on Walter Scott and John Galt. John Wilson: the Poet that Greenock Shut Up. 184pp. £4.00 *Southfields 3: City and Light* edited by Friel, Kinloch and Price.City-hop on the Southfields Trans-Cyberia Express: Glasgow to Tokyo via London, Lisbon, and Paris. Not forgetting Berlin, Istanbul, Moscow and Karachi (advanced reservation is advised for Paisley, Edinburgh and Stromness). New poems by: Donny O'Rourke, James McGonigal, Gael Turnbull, Joanne Limburg, Robin Fulton, Alan Riach, D. M. Black, Don Paterson, Robin Lindsay Wilson. Translations from the French of Emmanuel Moses, Turkish of Nazim Hikmet, Russian of Gennady Aygi. New prose by Donal McLaughlin, Moira Burgess and Kathleen Jamie. Paul Gordon on the poetry of Edwin Morgan, Jim Ferguson on Robert Tannahill, Bill Broady on Gustav Meyrink, and Robin Purves on Rimbaud and the City of Prose. Art by Gary Anderson and Tracy Mackenna. 166pp. £7.00 (current issue). Forthcoming: new format, *SoFi* 4.1 - Gael Turnbull on St Denys Garneau, A New Sequence by Penelope Shuttle, New Poetry by Peter McCarey, Cahal Dallat, Sheila Hamilton, Paul May, Drew Milne, Derick Thomson, Gary Allen, Desmond Graham, and Gordon Meade. Bill Broady on Dad and the National Health Service, Richard Price on Ian Hamilton Finlay, Peter McCarey on the Canonical Virus, John Manson on Louis Aragon (with translations from his later work). And more...c.64pp. £3. Cheques should be made payable to Southfields Press, 8 Richmond Rd, Staines, TW18 2AB.

TO MARK ITS 75TH ANNIVERSARY YEAR

THE CLASSICAL ASSOCIATION OF SCOTLAND (EDINBURGH & SE CENTRE)

PRESENTS

'THE CLASSICS AND SCOTTISH CULTURE – A CELEBRATION'

ON SATURDAY 27 SEPTEMBER 1997 IN EDINBURGH

SPEAKERS

IAIN CRICHTON SMITH   *ALLAN MASSIE*

THOMAS CLARK (nominated by *IAN HAMILTON FINLAY*)

ALEXANDER STODDART

CONFERENCE FEE £12 (£7.50 CONCESSIONS)   LUNCH (IF REQUIRED) £5.50

FOR DETAILS, PLEASE WRITE (WITH SAE) TO HON. SEC., CAS (E & SE), DEPT. OF CLASSICS, DAVID HUME TOWER, GEORGE SQUARE, EDINBURGH EH8 9JX

What Melarky Did

Patrick S. McEvoy

For almost as far back as he could remember, Tony had set his emotions by Colette's. When she was happy, he was adventurous. When she was angry, he begged forgiveness. When she cried, he felt tears stinging his eyes. Colette was the embodiment of Tony Harney's young dream. She was life, brightness; the focal point of an ethereal blissful future. When he held her hand there was a swagger in his step. He belonged to a universal fellowship which embraced all lovers from Erroll Flynn to Eamon Gibney, his next door neighbour, who had a real sweetheart over in Seaforde. Colette was his sacrament of sweet delight, and he was only ten years old.

Tony had been holding Colette's hand since his second day at school. On the first day his mother had brought him. He had held her hand in a vice-like grip at the entrance to the classroom. "Don't do that to your mother" Miss O'Driscoll had told him brusquely, causing him to choke back a sob as he took his allocated place on the hard bench along the wall. Since his mother didn't relish the two-mile walk morning and evening, Colette was recruited as his companion and guardian.

Colette lived in the white-washed house at the bottom of the hill which descended from Tony's home in Ballylenaghan. Her mother, a widow, carried out domestic duties for the local clergy. The woman's features demonstrated hard evidence of the common saying, "as ugly as a priest's housekeeper". But Colette was pretty. Tony met her every morning at the green gate, where his mother would say, "Take Colette's hand now; that's a good boy."

Tony had never been slow to take Colette's hand. It was warm and reassuring. At first there had been a few jibes from other boys who had no one to take their grubby hands; but these had never bothered Tony. He was proud to walk beside this big girl with the beautiful green eyes and burnished black hair brushed back from a snow-white forehead. Colette, five years his senior, was in Miss Kilroy's advanced class when he entered junior infants at Stonecastle Public Elementary School.

In those first early May mornings, corncrakes calling in the meadows had frightened Tony. Their sharpening cries sounded like scolding women. He had never heard of ventriloquism; didn't know that corncrakes could throw their voices, be everywhere at once. He felt surrounded, and gripped Colette's hand so tightly that she complained of cramp in her fingers. As summer progressed, Colette called him her "little gipsy boy", because of the way his skin had become bronzed by the sun. And when the older boys would toss the girls into the ditch coming home from school and try to take down their knickers, Colette would implore Tony to "hold on to my hand no matter what happens". Tony would clasp her hand ever more tightly and with such grim features that the aspiring molester would turn his attention elsewhere. At other times when brazen-faced girls threatened to remove Tony's trousers, Colette would have none of that either.

Colette was his special girl, and some nights before he swooned in sleep, he would drift across the future years to an appointed time when he would kiss her on the mouth and taste her sweet lips. And she would cry out, "We must stop here; it is just right." When they married they would resume more vigorous kissing in a little cottage like the one he shared with his parents. Colette would be baking fresh pancakes for tea and dipping them in a sweet sauce like his mother made every Saturday. He would be planting early potatoes in the garden and cultivating her special flower, the foxglove.

Whenever they took a short cut home by the old railway line, Colette would often pluck the purple globules and have him place one on each of her fingers. Then she would wiggle her hands above her head, sway her hips and declare, "I am Salome. I do the dance of the seven veils." She would slowly remove her cardigan and drop it to the ground. Her dress and petticoat would follow with all the seductiveness she could muster; and she would trip around in her vest and knickers. Tony thought she looked stupid when she carried on like this. He liked her better with her clothes on. He especially adored her in the pink floral dress when she agreed to be Maid Marian to his Robin Hood.

In the evenings after school they would go up to the old De Courcy castle. Tony would bring his makeshift bow and arrows, and go full pelt over the crumbling walls and up the musty stone stairs. When he reached the top he could see the British Army firing range across the bay, and wondered if he would ever play a part in driving them back to England where they belonged. But mostly he would gaze down at Colette sitting serenely in the evening sun, waiting for his whoop to warn her that the Sheriff of Nottingham was coming to kidnap her. Then he would come plunging recklessly down the steps to the rescue. He would gallop around her in diminishing circles, striking himself sharply on the backside as if he were on a horse, all the while releasing arrows at imaginary foes. When he was exhausted, she would bid him sit down and rest himself. Occasionally she would put her cool hand inside his jumper and exclaim, "You are boiling. You had better get cooled down before you go home." He would rest his head on her shoulder; and once she drew his face down and cradled it close to her breast until he thought he would smother. But he didn't resist because Colette quivered and seemed to like it.

When Colette reached fourteen, she left Stonecastle and travelled on the bus to the big school in the town. Tony would wait for her at the Miller's Corner, and they would walk home, hand in hand. It was around this time that she began to develop annoying habits. She was forever fixing her hair and whispering and giggling with other girls. What were the secrets that she wouldn't share with him? However, when she took his hand in her cool slender fingers he was happy again. He was still "Colette's right-hand man", according to those giddy girls who tittered so tiresomely.

When they went up to the castle, Colette would bring a tiny mirror and a pair of tweezers, and proceed to pluck her eyebrows. This was painful and brought tears to her eyes; and sometimes a little whispered swear-word from her red lips. Tony couldn't understand why she was punishing herself. He thought her eyebrows were perfect the way they were. She also began to complain that there were so few dances in the parish. Tony had never been to a dance, and didn't know what the big attraction was. Nor could she go to the pictures in the evening and afford the taxi fare home. So she went to the Saturday matinee and brought Tony. He wouldn't have called the king his uncle as he walked into the dimly lit auditorium and sat down on a velvet seat beside Colette. But the film was useless. There was no action, no shooting, no cowboys. It was all gentlemen and ladies engaged in dumb conversations and kissing. Tony noted that many of the couples around them were taking their cues from the screen. "May we kiss, Colette?" he inquired loudly.

"No! For Jesus sake shut your mouth. I'll be taken up for cradle-snatching."

One August evening as Tony waited for Colette by the green gate, an insolent youth with red hair and freckles seemed to emerge out of nowhere and caught Tony unawares. "Are you waiting for your sister again?"

"Colette is not my sister," Tony mumbled.

"Well, she's not your girl-friend, you little bugger. You're too young for trailing your wing."

Tony immediately hated this Freckles Melarky, as he was called by the local youth. Melarky came down every year from Belfast to spend the summer with his aunt in Magheramurray. The previous year he had become notorious when he brought two younger boys into chapel and robbed St Anthony's poor box. When the word got around, most parents forbade their children to have anything to do with him.

Melarky was persistant. The next evening he nabbed Tony again as he approached the laneway to the castle. "Where are you off to in such a hurry, shrimp?"

"De Courcy's Castle."

"That's not De Courcey's Castle; that's de courtin' castle," Melarky guffawed. "It's no place for a cub like you." Melarky Angelone, of Italian extraction from the Falls Road in Belfast, had been spying on Tony and Colette. He knew that the pair of them went up to the castle regularly. He wished to get Colette on her own, so he intimidated Tony. "I said clear off. Go play somewhere else, small fry."

"I have to meet someone up there."

"The big girl with the legs running right up to her arse. Now scram; or I'll kick you where it hurts."

The way was narrow. Tony had no choice but retreat. His immediate thought was to find another way up to his trysting place. This proved difficult. De Courcey had built the castle on a steep cliff with a sheer drop on three sides. It was accessible from only one direction. So after an hour spent clambering over jagged rocks and crawling under whin bushes, the agonised boy was forced to give up. He returned to the lane and waited behind the hedge at a spot he knew Colette would have to pass on her way home. It was dusk when she finally came into view with the dreaded Melarky beside her. They were chatting amiably, but she wasn't holding his hand. Colette was vindicated. She would always be his special girl.

The next evening Colette called for Tony to go to confession. They always went to the sacrament on the first Saturday of the month in preparation for communion on the Sunday morning. Tony delighted in going to confession with Colette. It seemed so grown-up. They usually chatted boisterously on the way, looking forward to the crack when Fr. Reynolds, who was deaf, would inadvertently disclose the sins of other penitents. When they had confessed their sins and said their penance, the pair would linger in the chapel in the hope of overhearing something hilarious. On one occasion they had heard Johnny McKay being reprimanded for eating sausages on a Friday. Another time they heard Mrs. Mohan complain loudly how her husband always tried to pull her knickers off her when she was washing the dishes. "Hit him a slap across the face with the dish cloth," Fr. Reynolds had retorted. Best of all they revelled in eavesdropping on Eddie Smith, who had a stammer. This sometimes made the priest so impatient that he would give poor Eddie the whole five decades of the rosary for his penance.

However, on this particular evening Colette was preoccupied. She took his hand, but scarcely spoke all the way to the chapel. While they waited their turn, Tony noticed that she kept fidgeting with her hair and nervously clearing her throat. When she was in the box, he heard Fr Reynolds say, "And did he try anything more than kiss you?" He couldn't make out her whispered reply; but he was certain that it had something to do with Freckles Melarky up at the castle.

Though he took her hand again on the way home, it didn't seem the same. Tony's heart was heavy. His parents remarked on him going to bed without supper, and him fasting in the morning. Tony went to early mass with his parents. He rushed up to communion and, back in his seat, buried his face in his hands in pretence of praying. Really he was peeping through his fingers, watching Colette go up the main aisle to receive the sacrament. He loved the cut of her hair at the nape of her neck; and watched expectantly to see her pink tongue shoot out to take the wafer. She had to return by the side aisle past the lounging Melarky, who hadn't been in time to get a seat. Tony could see that she reddened slightly as she passed the smirking youth.

When next they met, Tony was shy and hesitant to take her hand. In a matter of fact tone, she asked if he was "going up to the castle."

"I suppose so", he mumbled. He wanted to ask about Melarky, but hadn't the words. He was sure the freckled nuisance would put in an appearance. Tony's premonition proved too true. Just when he had got into the spirit of Robin Hood, shooting arrows from the top turret, he caught sight of the hated figure. Melarky sat close beside Colette and boldly put his arm around her. She didn't resist as she had when the big boys grabbed her coming from school. Soon he had her down on the grass tickling her, while she giggled stupidly. They ceased threshing about and went into a clinch. Tony's humiliation was complete when he saw that they were kissing. He stumbled down the dark stone stairway and raced off blindly along the steep path. He heard Colette call out, "Tony, wait for me." But he never looked round; just ran until he thought his heart would burst. He didn't stop until he reached a field known locally as the Black Park. There he lay face down on the coarse grass and sobbed dryly. His clawing fingers encircled a stone and he bashed it repeatedly off the ground, wishing it were pounding Melarky's skull.

Following this, Tony avoided Colette as much as possible. When she called for him he was always "away down the fields." That was all his mother knew about his whereabouts. Colette stopped calling; and when he saw her approaching with the inevitable Melarky, Tony would jump over the hedge and take to the fields to escape them. The fields were his sanctuary. He would lie on his back watching the butterflies flutter in pairs, and listen to the chink and tinkle of the robin and wren within the dark hedges. Was it possible that any of these creatures could be as forlorn as he?

Colette and Melarky became an item. They could be seen every evening, wrapped around each other on their way up to the castle. Everybody said they were "courting too strong." Tony's mother criticised Mrs. Herron for being lax in relation to her daughter's morals. "He'll pin her. That's what will happen," pronounced Molly Harney in the tone of one who knew about these things.

His father agreed. "Aye, he's a cute wee hoor from the city. He knows it's not for stirring his tea with."

These conversations sent Tony into the depths. What did his mother mean, he would "pin her?" He couldn't bear the thought of anyone hurting Colette. He would be her sad-eyed bridegroom always. His pain made him determined to find out more. One Friday evening after devotions he made his lonely way up to the castle and secluded himself near an opening on the first floor. He hadn't long to wait. As darkness fell he became aware of muffled laughter just below him. He craned his neck and could just make out two figures lying on the ground. Then he heard someone's hoarse whisper, "The best of friends must part and so must your two legs." A girl shrieked, half in protest, half in amusement. Tony edged his foot onto the parapet to get a better look. A stone became dislodged and he tumbled over the edge on top of the wrestling couple. Melarky swore. "Who the blazes are you" Colette was pulling her dress down over her knees. "It is you! You little bastard!" Melarky grabbed him by the jersey and placed three well aimed kicks on his backside before releasing him with a shove which sent Tony tumbling over the grass embankment. "Don't hurt him", he heard Colette plead, "he's only a youngster." So that was how she regarded him. He would never speak to her again.

A number of months had passed in Tony's confused and troubled life, when one Sunday his parents came home from mass in an agitated state.

It was all to do with a sermon preached by Fr Reynolds. Tony had paid little heed to the sermon. He had been watching for Colette as usual; but she had not been there, and he thought that odd. The parish priest had raised his voice and instructed the congregation that they must learn "to keep their scandalous noses out of other people's business."

"He has some cheek to talk to us like that," said his mother when they got home. "Aren't we keeping him where he is?"

"Sure the dogs are barking it in the street. Everyone knows what happened to the girl."

"We could see it coming", his mother went on with some satisfaction.

"Peter Grimes told me that the priest went to Melarky, and tried to get him to take responsibility. But the young waster defied him; said the priest could get stuffed."

"Poor creature. She'll have it up in Belfast, and they'll put it in the Good Shepherd."

"And probably keep her there too as a skivvy."

"God help her. She deserved better. Colette was a lovely girl. She was good to our Tony. Didn't she take him to school by the hand every day?"

It was Colette they were talking about. Something bad had happened to her; and it was all due to her association with that cursed Melarky. What had he done to her? Why were they whispering? Why didn't they want him to know? It must be something shameful. Perhaps he had given her T.B. City people were unhealthy; so grandad always said. Or maybe he had coaxed her to rob the poor box again, and she was in jail. He had to find out and there was only one person who could tell him. He had to be brave. So he went looking for Melarky. He went into the haggard behind the youth's house and hung around until the villain finally appeared.

"Well look who it is. Baa-lamb himself."

"What did you do to Colette?"

"What did I do to her?" Melarky sniggered. "Who told you to ask that, you wee snooper?"

"No one told me. I want to know myself. What did you do to her?"

"You want to know what I did to the big girl. Your education is lacking. Is that what it is? Come here and I will soon show you." He beckoned Tony to follow him behind a haystack. "This is what I done to her," he said, unzipping his trousers. "I poked her with this. Now scram, before I pish on you and you'll never grow another inch."

Tony wandered in torment through the meadows where he had romped so carefree with Colette only a few months earlier. A farmer was breaking the Sabbath, gathering in the last hay of the summer. Tony' throat was choking him. He would never pick foxgloves for Colette's fingers again, or sneak an apple from Grant's orchard and watch her white teeth sink into its juicy flesh. When he got home the house was empty. He dropped his trousers before the hall mirror, and examined the little thing between his legs. Would it ever become big and erect like Melarky's and be capable of hurting Colette? "Never! Never!" he shouted, and pinched it hard between his finger and thumb until he wailed.

Homage to the Carmina Gadelica: Carmichael's Book

The *Carmina Gadelica* is one of Scotland's great treasures. Although it is still in many ways a secret book it has the right to be named alongside the *Kalevala* or *Book of Songs*. The six leather-bound volumes that make up the *Carmina* were collected in the Highlands and the Western Isles by Alexander Carmichael, a government inspector who was also a native Gaelic speaker, (born on the isle of Lismore in 1832, died in Edinburgh 1912). Carmichael began his collecting in 1855, but the first and only volume of the *Carmina* to appear in his lifetime was not published until 1900. Carmichael had prepared a further five volumes for publication. These were edited by his grandson, James Carmichael Watson, and, after James was killed in action in 1942, by Angus Matheson. The sixth and final volume appeared over one hundred years after Carmichael's odyssey began.

The poems, blessings, prayers, curses and songs, all the oral lore and traditions which are gathered together in the *Carmina,* reach into the past, beyond the dark shadow of the Clearances, to speak and sing of the life and the beliefs, the feelings and the faith, of a people. Beneath the devout Christian imagery there is evidence of a plangent love of nature, an affection and reverence for the spirits of the forests, the glens and the seas.

Carmichael's Book, an anthology of poems written in response to the *Carmina Gadelica* will be published later this year. It is dedicated to the memory of Sorley MacLean, who celebrated Carmichael in his own poetry. Poets were invited to respond, in whatever way they chose, to Alexander Carmichael's life and work, to the book and the beautiful poetry it contains.

An exhibition of work by contemporary artists, made in response to the *Carmina,* will open at Highland Printmakers Gallery, Inverness, this winter and will subsequently tour the Highlands.

The following is a selection of poems by poets whose work is included in *Carmichael's Book.*

Alec Finlay (editor)
May 1997

Líos Mhor

A stranger finds a home in you, isle of broch,
Great Hunt of the Fianna,
Culdee haven, Lochlannoch outpost,
the high Churchman's palace.

Green isle in the great Gaelic deep,
your seabed limestone squeezed to air
by force that split the Earth as far as Shetland,
aligned the north with Scotland's west: you
sheltered Somerled, halfbreed Gael and Norse.

Líos Mhor, time-tides swell around your shores –
Glensanda's sides are torn by crumbling blasted sores,
while you, eye of the great ravine, weep early dew.

Here, among your undergrowth of youth,
Carmichael ran through bracken barefoot –
as faithful drones resounded Moluog's place,
words like autumn hazels gathered in his ear.
Now, the buzz of warplanes bursts your peace.

A white-tailed eagle rises from the kirk roof,
flails away from winter's cropless croft subsiding
imperceptibly to unfarmed bogland.

But green isle, see how your songs go with him,
weaving outward, till among the many echoes,
they find a narrow pass, a tidal seaward channel,
to the scattered, soulless world.

Robert Alan Jamieson

Gun Athair Ann

Aig amannan bidh mi a' smaoineachadh
nach eil sa chultar seo a th' againn
ach dòigh air bodaich a mholadh – cuid dhiubh
marbh a cheana, ciud aig uchd a' bhàis.

Carson a dh'iarr thu dàn orm, Alasdair
Mhic Iain, bhiodh na leisgeul airson bodach
eile mholadh? Fàgaidh mi ri càch
a bhith air bhoile sireadh athraichean

ùra ni nas eifeachdaich' na sgrìobh iad,
mar nach robh 'n t-athair ceart a' fòghnadh dhaibh.
Chan fhaca mi san teaghlach ach blàr-catha
a fhuair mi às gun dùil a'm ris, 's a' chasgairt

sin a' dol air adhart air cùl mo ghuaillean
(is dòcha nach do chuireadh stad oirre fhathast).
Thachair mi ris a' chànain seo mar neach
a b' fheudar dha teicheadh bho bhaile, ghlac

an trean' a b' fhaisg' a fhuair e anns an stèisean,
gun fheòrachadh mu ainm a' chompanaidh
no mun cheann-ùidh', eadhon gun chothrom fhaotainn
an ticead iomchaidh cheannach 'son a thurais.

Air neo (math dh'fhaodte) nuair a bhriseadh long,
mar cudeigin nach d' rinn ach snàmh, 's ùpraid
is gaoir na cuid a bhàthadh air a chùl,
a thachair ri crios-teasairginn sa mhuir

's a fhuair gu tìr leis. Ach dh'fheòraich na daoin'
a choinnich ris san tràigh ciod e an dlighe
a bh' aige air, 's co thuirt gum faodadh e
ùisneachadh. Gu dearbh, cha do fhreagair mi

gur ann bho Alasdair Mhic Ghille Mhicheil
a fhuair mi e! Thairg thu athair eile
dhomh: ach thuirt Tsvetaeva gur iad
mic na màthar an fheadhainn as laoiche.

Cha ghiùlain sinn ainmean ar màthraichean:
's an tosd na dhàn aig mòran dhiubh, chan abrainn
gu faigh sinn bhuap' a' chainnt, oir cha bhiodh innt'
ach fearg shàmhach mar talamh a' crith, no rùcail

tàirneanaich 's i fad air falbh. Cha robh
an t-ainm a thugadh dhomh lem athair ach
na àite bàn, na fhàsalachd a theab mi
tuiteam ann. Seall air na h-uirsgeulan!

Thubhairt caraid ann am Barcelona
a bhios a' sgrìobhadh nobhailean, gun d' rinn
bana-sgoilear Fhrangach dealachadh
eadar dà sheorsa sgrìobhaichean: a' chuid

a ni an athraichean dligheach a dhiùltadh,
's a' chuid nach eil fhios aca co an athair.
Tha mise buntainn don an dàrna seòrs'.
Mar sin is ionmhainn leam na h-uirsgeulan.

Tha iomadh dòigh air gineamhainn ri fhaighinn
annta. Faodaidh osag boireannach
a thorrachadh, no port, no aingeal, ciùbhran
mìn is draoidheachd ann, no sealladh, ìomhaigh

a thachras rith' air uachdar linne, guth
nan duilleag, neul san adhar, eun a bheir
faillean ùr na ghob. Ma dh'fheòraicheas
tu cò 'n t-athair a bh' agam, b' annsa leam

tachartas mar seo a thaghadh. Alasdair,
cha do nochd thu riamh ach coibhneas rium,
ach eadhon air do sgàth chan aithnich mi
dìlseachdan no athraichean nach fhìor.

Christopher Whyte

Absence of a Father

Sometimes I think
our culture is just
a pretext for praising old men:
some of them dead already, some on the verge of death.

So Alasdair, why have you asked for a poem
that would be a pretext for praising
one more old man? I will leave others
to search frenziedly for new fathers

who can validate what they have written
as if their real father weren't enough.
All I saw in the family was a battlefield
I escaped from without expecting to, and that slaughter

still going on behind my shoulders
(it may not have been put a stop to yet).
I came upon this language like someone
who has to flee a city, and who catches

the train nearest to him in the station
without asking the name of the company
or the destination, without even getting
a chance to buy the right ticket for the journey.

Or else, perhaps, in a shipwreck,
like someone who just kept swimming, behind him
the fighting and shouts of the people who drowned,
then came upon a lifesaver in the sea

*and reached land with its help. But the people
I met on the beach asked me what right I had
to it, and who had told me
I could use it. I didn't answer*

*that I got it from Alasdair Carmichael!
You want to foist another father
on me, but Tsvetaeva has said
that mother's sons are better than father's.*

*We do not carry our mother's names.
Silence is the destiny of many of them.
I would not even say we get speech from them –
it could only be silent anger like an earthquake*

*or the rumble of distant thunder. The name
my father gave me was merely a white space,
an emptiness I almost fell into.
Look at the old tales!*

*A friend in Barcelona
who writes novels, told me
that a French woman, a scholar, divides
writers into two categories:*

*those who deny their rightful fathers
and those who don't know who their father was.
I belong to the second group.
That is why I love the old stories.*

*So many ways of generating can be found
in them. A breeze can make a woman
pregnant, a tune, an angel, a fine
drizzle with magic in it, a look, the image*

*she encounters on the surface of a pool,
the voice of foliage, a cloud in the sky, a bird
with a fresh sprig in its beak. If you ask
who my father was, I would prefer*

*to choose one of these incidents.
You have never been other than kind to me,
Alasdair, but even for your sake I will not
acknowledge either false loyalties or fathers.*

Christopher Whyte

The Swan

Ah a honking, oh a honking!
Ah a honking, oh a honking!
Ah a honking, oh a honking!
Voice of the swan, voice of the bird.

Voice of the swan and she in the fog,
Voice of the swan crying aloud,
Voice of the swan in the morning,
Voice of the swan on the bog-pool.

Voice of the swan in the channel,
Voice of the swan in the cold,
Voice of the swan and in hard straits,
Voice of the swan in the channel.

My one foot black,
my one foot black,
my one foot black
      and marching;
my one foot black
at the stream's mouth,
the other one fumbling
      wounded.

Version after 'An Eala', Carmina Gadelica *by Harry Gilonis*

Eolas Airson Graidh

Tri cnamhan seann-duine
An deigh an creann a uaigh.

Leugh mi an eòlas airson gràidh
airson faighinn a mach
ciamar a gheibhinn eòlas air do gràidh-s
dh' fhoignich mo dhomh fhìn
an deidhinn a chladhach ann an cladh
air do sgàth
Cha deidheadh.

Ligidh mi dha na mairbh cadal
gu sàmhach anns an uaigh
ged a bhiodh do ghaol ormsa
nam measg.

Anne Frater

A Spell for Love

Three bones of an old man
Removed from the grave.

I read the spell for love
to find out
how I could get to know your love;
I asked myself
if I would go digging in a graveyard
for your sake.

No.

I will let the dead sleep
peacefully in the grave
although your love for me
might be among them.

Anne Frater

Jetsam

Wrecked
after the trip to market

a skiff smashed to matchsticks
across the rocks

of Coll.
Among the littered you lay still

in your soaked linen shirt
the heart stirred

and, mouth to mouth
I could taste your breath

so, my lad
I hauled you home to bed

nursed you back to life
of course, in love

followed you to the furthest
westerly coast

we bred, throve.
I don't say nothing was lost.

Elizabeth James

beannachd

beannachd na grèine, beannachd an uisge
solus na làn-ghealaich air achadh reòta

blessing

*the blessing of the sun, the blessing of the water
light of the full moon on a frosty field*

Kevin MacNeil

Isabel of Bunessan, Mull

Isabel,
You knew the plants
you knew of the darkness
in the wounds we carry,
the sickness
we must know and love.
And with no less love.
you could find
the simple, the herb
the words.

You found the words
to carry our darkness
to pentrate it
to look at it
and hold it
gently, with love
then, return it
to the sea
*she herself
the best one
to bear it
the great surging sea.*

Jayne Wilding

St. Fillan's Day

the January day
day of St. Fillan's fair
day no work's done in the mill
day the wheel doesn't turn
day of the big snowfall
day they can't mend the roof
day to stop the traffic

day of silence
day of a first cry
day to give birth
to the snow child
to the lad of winter
on a day of ice
he warms the stream

lucky Saturday
day to hear his bell
day to see it flying
day of a newborn son
a new sword for Scotland
boy from my bones
on the day of my Fillan.

Valerie Gillies

Near Sioc Dubh, South Uist

The roof beams have fed the flame,

the walls bowed to the wind

and the pasture made welcome the heather.

Where the drove road scarred the hill

is only a caress of shadow, nearly healed.

Even the old don't weep any more

or the children go to bed hungry.

Silence inhabits the glen.

Remembering is our tomorrow.

Forgetting, what won't come again.

Gael Turnbull

Faisg air Sioc Dubh, Uibhist a deas

Bhiadh na sparran an lasair,

lùb na ballachan rus a' ghaoith,

's rinn an t-ionaltradh furan ris an fhraoch.

Chan eil, far na sgròb rathad dròbha an cnoc,

ach suathadh faileis, slàn, cha mhòr.

Chan eil an sean fhèin a' gul a-nis

no a' chlann a' dol acrach dhan leabaidh.

Ghabh samchair an gleann.

'S e cuimhne a chumail tha romhainn.

'S dìochuimhneachadh, an nì nach till.

Translation of 'Near Sioc Dubh, South Uist' by Maoilios Caimbeul

A Walk Through the Gaelic Alphabet

Walking through the same trees
though in a different language
wading in the long river running
of words
among the hawthorn, birch and alder
the same words
wych elm, bramble, ivy
gorse of the thousand swords
no new words.
On the hill slope
there is oak and ash there is elder,
willow in the damp places
everywhere
dwarf, goat, crack, white willow
trees that make the same words.
Then there is larch
and pine of the bare hill
ranked now in squares
words in a new order.

*(Each letter of the Gaelic alphabet is
represented by a different species of tree.)*

Angus Dunn

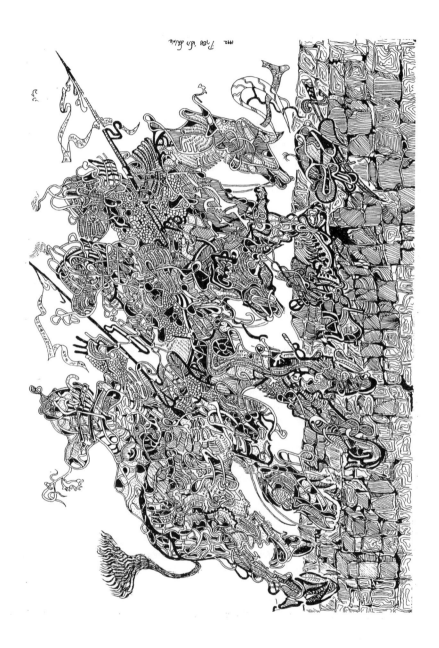

Illustration by Robin Spark

Eskimo

Bill Duncan

A paddle, a mitt, a boot: all that remain in Dundee Museum to remind visitors of the extraordinary story of the Eskimo who arrived in Dundee under bizarre circumstances and made our city his home for two short years. The story of Chikanuk, the Sinderins Eskimo, is recalled by Bessie Gibson, the 103 year old daughter of Rab, one of the men who discovered Chikanuk that winter morning in 1903 . . .

Bessie told her story to Bill Duncan, who translated it into English.

A cold December day in the Baltic Dock, and my father and his two mates were unloading horse carcasses onto the whaler 'Narwhal'. Taking a break from this strenuous work, something caught the eye of one of the men, and the three went to investigate. They were astounded to discover the form of an Eskimo, slumped semi-conscious in his kayak.

The fellows assisted the man into a dockside hostelry and, presently revived by the hearty company and flowing spirits, Chikanuk held the circle of dockers in thrall with his tale, communicated to the men by my father's mate, a fluent Inuit-speaking cabinet-maker from Lochee. Caught on a stray current during an Arctic storm, Chikanuk was carried far from that dazzling but inhospitable realm, through nights of groaning bergs and gnashing floes, through blinding Aurorae and howling blizzards, to awake into a fine Dundee morning.

There being no whaling ship voyaging to the Eskimo's homelands until the departure of 'The Baleena' the following Spring, Chikanuk took up lodgings with a harpooner in Tait's Lane. Chic soon became something of a celebrity in the West End, where the folk were not slow to take the appealing fellow to their hearts. He quickly became an attraction in the crowded Hawkhill taverns, regaling the appreciative companies with his store of Eskimo legend and folksongs. His rendition of 'The Walrus and the Maiden', yodelled in Inuit and broken Dundonian, was a particular favourite which delighted the ears of many. To see Chikanuk in the Empress Ballroom on a Saturday night, waltzing in full Arctic regalia, was indeed an unforgettable experience.

Being of an exceptionally cheerful and gregarious disposition, Chikanuk became involved in a wide range of community affairs, an especial highlight being his visits to local primary schools. What finer visual aid could be presented to children studying the Arctic than a live Eskimo in the classroom? Ever eager to entertain and delight, Chic would share with the children his beloved repertoire of Arctic lore. Bessie recalls, as a youngster in Hawkhill Primary, Chikanuk playing a nose-flute of his own invention, ingeniously fashioned from the tusk of a walrus. His performance of 'The Boy, the Girl and the Igloo', complete with dance and mime, delighted the young charges in Miss Simpson's Primary 7. Some of the more immoderate of Chic's illustrative actions, however, left Miss Simpson (who declined Chikanuk's spirited invocations to participate) shaking and ashen-faced.

A particular favourite among Chikanuk's young audience in Blackness Primary was "A Boy and his Beluga", an Inuit whale-flensing song, delivered with stupendous gusto, while four of his young charges acted out mysterious rituals under an old blanket, representing the skin of the Leviathan. The same children were no less delighted when, on arrival in the playground one January morning after an unexpected snowfall, they discovered an enormous, expertly-built igloo. Such was the degree of skill exercised in the edifice's construction that it served for some days as a makeshift classroom when burst pipes rendered the Primary 6 classroom inoperative.

With the passing of the seasons and with Chic's apparently happy adoption of Dundee, some folk began to see the Eskimo as a permanent feature of Dundee's West End. Alas, with the onset of a second winter, Chikanuk's heart was pining for his frozen homelands. One morning he gazed wistfully at the slowly falling snowflakes, drifting around the expertly-fashioned walrus he had built in the backies for the amusement of the bairns. The next morning he was gone, leaving nothing but a paddle, a mitt, a boot, a host of happy memories and the pair of scrimshaw penguins which, to this day, have pride of place on my mantelpiece.

Tourist boom after Oscars

Delighted tourism chiefs today predicted a boom in the number of people visiting Scotland following the success of Danny Boyle's film *Trainspotting* at last night's Oscars.

The film, the savage tale of the 90s heroin addict Mark Renton, won a total of five Oscars.

Scottish Tourist Board Chief Executive Derek Reid said, "If there had been an Oscar for Best Supporting Country, I'm sure Scotland would have picked it up. We're delighted *Trainspotting* has achieved this recognition for Scotland. Its portrayal of our scenery and heritage will undoubtedly provide a significant boost to a tourism industry worth £2 billion annually to the Scottish economy."

Ewan McGregor's stirring portrayal of Mark Renton, against a stunning backdrop of some of Scotland's most striking settings and heroic characters, also helped persuade more Britons to holiday at home last year, according to the STB.

More Cat Tortures

Another cat has been found tortured in Kirkfield, Dundee. Cats in the area have been subjected to systematic cruelty by gangs of children.

Flossie was found near the Mill Burn with a rope round her neck and was reckoned by R.S.P.C.A. officers to have been hanging there for at least two days. Miraculously, she survived her ordeal and has been re-united with her owner. She received 20 stitches to a neck wound.

An R.S.P.C.A. officer said "Many cats go missing in this area. 25 have been reported missing in the last month." A local resident who declined to be named said "Last Tuesday I heard wailing and laughter and went out to investigate. I caught a gang of four children, about 8-10 years old, trying to put a noose around a cat's neck and had to chase them away. Two of them were wearing stout gloves, another was holding a bag and the other one was uncoiling a length of rope. They seemed organised and knew what they were doing." His wife said "Some nights around here the noise is awful. The screeching and yowling drifts up from the burn on a quiet evening and I've taken to wearing ear-plugs to get a night's sleep."

A spokesman for Tayside Police said "We are aware of this problem in the Kirkfield area. It appears to be a trend among youngsters there at the moment. We would ask all cat owners to keep their pets in as much as possible and also request parents to check on the whereabouts of their children during the school holiday period. We are doing all we can to stamp out this unpleasant practise."

Birling Boab

I enjoy the letters from correspondents reminiscing about the worthies of Dundee yesteryear.

I, too, am an old-timer and am saddened by the lack of personalities on today's Dundee scene.

Where is today's equivalent of Birling Boab, the Polepark street dancer of the 1930s ?

Many a long summer evening we would gather round in the streets as Birling Boab wove his magic.

There were no 'ghetto blasters' (as my teenage grandson calls his wireless) or 'Top of the Pops' in those days, but the simple accompaniment of whistling and banging on biscuit tins did us fine!

Aye, even the memory of Boab, a fine figure of a man in his undertaker's coat, Black watch trews and white spats, is enough to raise a smile.

Old Timer, Hawkhill

Memories of Joey

Do any of your older readers recall Joey, the Royal Arch pigeon, who for many years strutted proudly around that esteemed structure, as if it had been built for him alone?

My family and I have many happy memories of Joey, most notably the Ne'er Day jaunts we made especially to feed and water him.

To see him picking happily away at some home-made dumpling was a joy to behold.

And when I recall the tears of my children when poor Joey was found dead one morning on the tramlines at the Arch.

Whatever happened to the simple pleasures of yesteryear?

Old Timer, Hawkhill

Dead Hens Mystery

Mystery surrounds the gruesome discovery of the partially burned bodies of six hens on a disused road bordering Dundee's Blackfield estate.

The bodies of the six birds were found by Blackfield Avenue resident Thomas Douglas as he walked his dog in Pitkerr Road.

Three black hens had been left at the side of the road – two had their legs chopped off. The charred remains of the three beheaded white hens were lying in the ashes of a bonfire.

"I think the fire was lit on Tuesday night", said Mr. Douglas. "My wife noticed a smell of burning and heard laughter and squawking. I went to investigate but I couldn't see anyone".

Dundee District Council Environmental Health Department has been alerted. A spokesman from Tayside Police advised householders in the area to exercise especial vigilance over their hens: "Whoever did this could strike again".

Joey and Bessie

Well do I remember Joey, the Royal arch pigeon. I wonder if Old Timer realises that not one, but two pigeons lived in the Royal Arch for many years?

Joey, a fine figure of a bird, frequented the upper recesses of the structure for seventeen years, later being joined by a mate.

Joey and Bessie fed mainly on the crusts of pies and bridies left by local tram crews, who were not slow to take the appealing couple to their hearts. Old Timer is correct in pointing out that Joey met his sad end on the tramlines. Shortly after, Bessie flew off, never to be seen again.

Not surprisingly, the birds attracted a fair deal of local attention and stories surrounding them became exaggerated.

One account states that the birds flew off the day the Arch was demolished, but is quite wrong. This version can still be heard in a little known Lochee folk song.

May I say how much I enjoy being transported by your correspondents to the innocent pleasures of Dundee's past?

Aye, even the pigeons were characters in those days!

Inky Wingham, Tait's Lane

Explanatory Note

The preceeding items play havoc with the distinction between urban myth, wild imaginings and fact. Some are total fabrications, which nevertheless appeared in local newspapers and were thus immediately invested with the status of Truth. My sister-in-law, when reading in Dundee's "Evening Telegraph" letter page about Birling Boab (who never existed) asserted "Eh mind o' him." Two of the articles push the latent craziness of local news a little too far, nudging it from the merely ridiculous into the bizarre. The 'Pigeon' letters are part of a lengthy correspondence which I had with myself. I replied to my own letters, one of which included the lyrics of the "little-known Lochee folk song". The subject matter is entirely invented, claiming that one of the pigeons sported a wooden leg fashioned from timbers reclaimed from the Tay Bridge Disaster. Needless to say, my sister-in-law knows someone whose mother remembers the pigeon. The 'Tourist boom after Oscars' article is a straight reproduction of one which appeared recently; the only change is my substitution of references to "Trainspotting" everytime "Braveheart" was referred to in the original.[1]

---

1. Not all of this is necessarily true.

Reviews

Views From the Periphery

Peripheral Visions: Images of Nationhood in Contemporary British Fiction, Ian Bell (ed.), University of Wales Press, £12.95; *Poetry in the British Isles: Non-Metropolitan Perspectives*, Hans-Werner Ludwig & Lothar Fietz (eds.), University of Wales Press, £14.95; *Seeking Mr Hyde: Studies in Robert Louis Stevenson, Symbolism and the Pre-Modern*, Tom Hubbard, Peter Lang, Scottish Studies Vol. 18, DM45; *Studies in Scottish Fiction: 1945 to the Present*, Susanne Hagemann (ed.), Peter Lang, Scottish Studies Vol. 19, DM84.

These four thoroughly-academic books are all concerned with literary perspectives at the periphery, albeit in geographical terms, or in terms of contesting the symbolic hegemony of the centre. But as they are all collections of essays, this review will necessarily have to be brutally selective: certain articles will inevitably appeal or intrigue more than others.

Bell's book addresses itself in general terms to the politics of place and writing. As Bell says himself in his Introduction:

> By means of its extensive testimony to lived experience, the novel seems to offer the possibility of exploring local communities and marginalised identities in the most elaborate ways (p.2).

Steven Knight's piece on regional crime fiction was interesting. He argues that crime writers have either got to construct an imaginary setting for their crime, or locate it in a real setting, and celebrate it. As he correctly says:

> Place and region as issues and as signs are deep-laid voices of meaning in crime fiction, especially (as readers of Sherlock Holmes will know) when they are apparently most silent (p.28).

Dorothy McMillan's essay on Scottish fiction observes that it is all but impossible for local writers to avoid the question of national identity. But in talking about Iain Banks' novel *The Crow Road*, a striking metaphor appears:

> Glass wonderfully figures the unity in diversity to which the idea of the nation aspires. It is a compound of disparate naturally occurring substances which behaves as a solid though it has many of the properties of a liquid... The end product may shatter at a sound, yet another version of it may provide the material for the nose-cone of a rocket (p.90).

Of the other pieces, Ken Worpole gives a compelling account of London writers' perennial fascination with "Outcast London", and the strong traditions of melodrama, the music-hall, and cosmopolitanism which pervade its fiction. This collection ends with a passionate and powerful essay by George Wootton arguing that the marginal literature is not that from the geographical peripheries, but that which writes about *social* relations, the *relations of production* which affect personal life. He asks: who remembers Frank Owen? Well, this reviewer does, and it is a pleasure to see novels like *The Ragged-Trousered Philanthropists* and Pat Barker's *Union Street* being discussed seriously again.

The Ludwig and Fietz volume also addresses poetry's relationship to place. It starts with a brilliant polemical preface by Christopher Harvie, who expands on the fact that the counter-attack on the 1979 Devolution Referendum debacle in Scotland was *literary*. M.Wynn Thomas takes on the thorny question of what is the appropriate language for a Welsh poet. As he shows, poets like Tony Conran and Jeremy Hooker successfully write in English *and* express Welsh identity by tapping into the deep wells of an old Welsh grammar and syntax. Kimpel's article on Scottish poetry shows how Sorley MacLean's 'Hallaig', Norman MacCaig's 'A Man in Assynt', and Edwin Morgan's 'Glasgow Green' all seem to successfully reinvent Scotland without the need to find a common national identity in three different places. They each find diversity in one place which is full of deep personal meaning. Of the remaining articles, the one which stands out is that by Raymond Hargreaves on the Leeds poetry of Tony Harrison, with its strong regional, class and political reverberations, and preoccupations with the problems of social mobility. As the perspicacious Hargreaves observes, Harrison's is a true voice, but it's a voice from the terraces of Elland Road.

Tom Hubbard's book consists of his interconnecting series of four essays on RLS. This is a book strictly for the Stevenson specialist. Hubbard, in a rather grating epigrammatic style, draws attention to the "compressed dualities" in his novels, the "hellish energies" and "attractive villains". He discusses Stevenson's "carnivilisation", and its propensity to subvert the Calvinism of the Edimbourgeoisie, and, with the help of Jung, delves into the Faustian themes of transformation, deformation and rejuvenation in his work. It is all very scholarly, somewhat obscurantist, and throttles the word "chthonic" to death.

Finally, to Hagemann's collection of essays on postwar Scottish fiction, a book which proved far and away the most interesting of the four under review. In a typically incisive introductory essay, Douglas Gifford sets the tone for the rest of this volume. He says:

> In essence I argue that a new grouping of writers is emerging who refuse to accept the old polarities, and who create in their novels an interlocking and interweaving of ideas which refuses to accept the premises of Scottish writing in its previously polarized twentieth century attitudes (p.18).

These new novelists achieve this by asserting a Scottish identity which is entire rather than fragmented, universal rather than parochial, synthetic rather than regional, extrovert rather than introvert, feminist rather than masculinist, optimistic rather than pessimistic, magic rather than mundane. Yet, as Gifford correctly points out, these contemporary writers *do* have a sense of Scottish identity, they *do* refer to ". . . a sub-text of tradition, legend and myth, with a deliberate intention to connect contemporary and past Scotlands" (p.38). The point is that they do it in *their* terms, they seek *their* new identities, in a sophisticated, principled and highly imaginative manner. This is a seminal essay, the best thing the author, or

anybody else, has written about post-1979 Scottish fiction thus far.

Alan Riach follows with an essay "Orphans and their Ancestors in Popular Scottish Fiction". I knew it was only a matter of time before someone deconstructed Lobey Dosser. Is nothing sacred? And Riach asserts that the cartoon-strip character, The Bogie Man, is "...an essential text of late twentieth-century Scottish literary culture" (p.72). Gie's peace. Malzahn and Sellin both provide essays on Robin Jenkins, on *The Thistle and the Grail*, and *A Very Scotch Affair* respectively. We learn that the truth in Jenkins' fiction, just as in real life, is far from simple; that his characters, just as in reality, are imperfect; and that for all his complaining about his mundane surroundings, his writing demonstrably constitutes remarkable literature. I think that some of us suspected that already. Monnickendam follows with a piece on "Landscape in the Fiction of Jessie Kesson". While this essay is perceptive about Kesson, the import of authorities such as Dekker and Said serve only to mystify the author's purpose. Next is Christopher MacLachlan on 'Muriel Spark and Gothic'. This is an insightful and original essay which argues convincingly that the metaphysical fears which are central to Spark's fiction can be illuminated by referring to the central preoccupations of "Gothic" writing with the supernatural, the numinous, the unknoweable – which is not the same as saying that Spark is a Gothic writer. What both Spark and the Gothic do is threaten commonsense understandings of the world.

Carolan-Brozy and Hagemann write about Scotland as reflected in the Canadian novelist Margaret Laurence's *The Diviners*. Essentially, what we learn is that the Canadian vision is of a prelapsarian Scotland. This seems to me to say more about the absence of a Canadian identity than to illuminate ours. The ubiquitous Christopher Harvie follows on North Sea Oil and Scottish culture, pointing out that with the significant exception of McGrath's *The Stag, The Cheviot, and the Black, Black Oil*, the 1970s in Scotland saw much more political than cultural activity. The offshore oil industry did not inspire any literary representation. Yet in the 1980s, the position is quite reversed – an anomaly also noted by Douglas Gifford. Keith Dixon follows with an overdue rehabilitation of Willie McIlvanney. Everybody knows the lacunas in McIlvanney's fiction, but few appreciate the strengths of his prose, informed as it is by "...a moral seriousness, a strongly didactic and, once again, unfashionable conviction about what is right and what is wrong: community values are unreservedly endorsed: violence against the weak or robbing the poor are equally unreservedly condemned; but those who commit these acts are portrayed as neither monsters, nor fairies – just people" (p.196).

Margaret Pittin continues with an excellent trace of the ambiguities, elusivenesses and fantasies of Alasdair Gray – alas, without his wit. Ian Bell follows with a convincing essay on contemporary attempts to imagine Scottish identity through a series of characters living alienated and disjointed lives, through a critique of popular and indeed populist historiography and literature. Next is Simon Baker on James Kelman's "urban realism" as illustrated through the prism of Welsh fiction. While Baker is astute on Kelman, there is not much light refracted from Wales. Alan Freeman continues with a somewhat, likesay, heavy piece on Irvine Welsh and *Trainspotting*, and the volume concludes with Ian Campbell showing how George Mackay Brown transcends the local in *Beside the Ocean of Time*.

These four books constitute a mixed bag, then, and will appeal to academic and lit. crit. audiences rather than the general reader. In general terms, each justifies its purpose, if sometimes encumbered with a heavy academic baggage train. But many of the essays are both insightful and original. An encouraging theme to emerge clearly from all four is that a sense of place, both at a national and regional level, is still important to poets and novelists in these islands. What is even more encouraging is that both kinds of writers seem to have broken free from the stereotyped, falsely-consensual, reactionary and sentimental forms of local and national literary consciousness supplied by the dominant ideology of the past. *Seán Damer*

Uncountable Bodies

The Eagle and the Crow, T. Halikowska/G. Hyde (eds.), Serpent's Tail, £9.99; *The Tiger Garden, A Book of Writer's Dreams*, N. Royle (ed.), Serpent's Tail, £9.99; *Children of Albion Rovers*, K. Williamson (ed.), Canongate, £8.99.

To be honest, how much do we know about Poland? The Pope is Polish, fair enough, but beyond that . . . ? *The Eagle and the Crow*, a collection of modern Polish short stories, is a delightful piece of European literature that leads us over the Scottish borders to a nearby country that seems more exotic to us than the all too familiar US. The Polish language bears the mark of minority status and thus it is no surprise that its literary works are largely excluded from the literary canon. Compiled by two academics who come from the background of Comparative Literature and Translation Studies, *The Eagle and the Crow* is an important work in that it brings Eastern European art and history closer to us.

Symbolising Poland's national emblems the title expresses the book's concern: its stories are about past and present, nationhood and communism, proud glory and the uncountable bodies which haunt Poland's history. Many are historical in that you cannot ignore the component of 'Zeitgeist' in them, the historical avalanches that shaped Polish experience – occupations, the Holocaust, Communism, Solidarnozs. Unsentimentally disturbing is Tadeuz Borowski's 'This Way for the Gas, Ladies and Gentlemen'. It depicts a scene in a concentration camp that makes you wonder if it did not influence various shots in Spielberg's *Schindler's List*. Hanna Krall ghost-writes the tale of a female Holocaust survivor and adapts it for action-hungry Hollywood, Pawel Huelle tells the story of Mennonites in Poland, and in Stefan Chwin's 'The Touch' a little girl meets Stalin. Other stories, such as Bruno Schulz's and Witold Gombrowicz's, are steeped in Romanticism and seem timeless in their evocation of a shabby provincial gentry and poor peasantry. 'Dinner at Countess Kotlubay's' – an absurd fantasy – reminded me of Karen Blixen's *Babette's Feast* and draws the unusual connection between a vegetarian feast and the death of a peasant boy called Cauliflower. You also find a new science-fiction tale by internationally acclaimed Stanislaw Lem and witty similes by Poland's foremost philosophers and satirists. Slawomir Mrozek's story about a giant inflatable elephant in Warsaw Zoo which is blown away and thus destroys children's belief in 'fundamental truths' (in this case big grey animals), is so harmlessly cute you want to read it aloud. And there is Kolakowski's swift interpretation of the Bible:

> Plot: The psalmist writes about God: 'He hath smitten Egypt with her firstborn; for His mercy endureth for ever'. And he hath cast Pharao with his horde into the Red Sea; for His mercy endureth for ever.' Question: What do Egypt and Pharao think about the mercy of God? Moral: mercy and benevolence cannot exist for everyone. When using these words, we should always say whom they are for. And when we confer benevolence upon whole nations, we should first of all ask them what they think of our benevolence. For example, Egypt.

I consider *The Eagle and the Crow* a strong book, able to provide sources for in-depth study as well as enjoyable bed-time reading, and highly recommended to all those interested in Eastern European literature.

> I was sitting on a bench in a dark vestibule. Backstage somewhere? I'm not sure. But I was sitting on a bench and there was a man sitting to my left. When I looked again I saw it was Robert Browning. He was disgruntled about something, though he said nothing. I looked down and noticed he had no right leg and that I was annoying him more by sitting on his empty trouser leg.

This is Michael Ondaatje's dream, and if you would like to learn more about the nocturnal experiences of the not so rich, but 'intellectual and famous', have a look at *The Tiger Garden, A Book of Writer's Dreams*. Here you find everything – from nightmares, recurring haunting images, children's dreams, to poetic dreams and dream-poems such as the one by Iain Crichton Smith. Although these intimate revelations by more than 200 international artists make for bed-time reading and a handy gift on the birthday table, the book did not have much personal relevance for me. Of course the validity of Freud's assumptions about dreaming and the creative process of writing cannot be doubted here. Yet I find reading about other people's dreams, even those of celebrities, slightly voyeuristic, sensational . . . and above all, let's face it, boring. For those maybe more informed than me here's a 'whistle stop tour' through the Tiger Garden: "Madison Smart Bell rides an elevator with Bill Clinton, who has grown a beard, while Rupert Thomson comes face to face with Margaret Thatcher, who hasn't. Gary Indiana's mother, meanwhile, is going out with Hitler. Michèle Roberts climbs into a microlight with a couple of nuns, but Jan Morris takes the controls herself and flies solo – her only problem is ground control talking in Mongolian. Jonathan Coe's reunion gig is already a total disaster by the time his keyboard starts turning into a pizza. A S Byatt finds herself on a terrace overlooking a lawn previously dreamt by Iris Murdoch, who appears, looking surprisingly pink. Donna Tartt watches while brains are dished up with a French sauce and herb garnish – human brains, that is, William Wharton watches his friends devoured by lions, and Fay Weldon has a brush with death on a mountain road."

A controversial new publication is the *Children of Albion Rovers* by Canongate's imprint Rebel Inc. It's a collection of short stories by young urban writers, all icons of the recently emerged acid scene, displaying a large range of talents from Scotland. The link to football – the Albion Rovers dream team – and clever marketing immediately 'image' the book as rebellious counter-literature. The new voices of the *Children of Albion Rovers* are indeed dazzling and enticing. Riding on the recent success wave of urban realism, the book is a product of 90s Britain and an addition to the contemporary hip-rave-techno scene. In their graphic depiction and choice of themes, the authors are out to shock and provoke. Raves, drugs, alcohol and sex are the main topics, with all the accompanying descriptions of their bodily effects on bowels and genitals. Plunging you right into the seemingly rather bleak and monotonous existence of Scottish urban youngsters, the stories reveal a good deal of perverse humour, yet often merely scratch their lives without getting to the core of the characters. A pity!

If you enjoy reading about dope, brawls and booze, however, this book is an absolute must! Rich with local colour and references to real events and people, it can be read as a portrait of Scottish youth culture. Take for example Laura Hird's 'The Dilating Pupil', in which a male teacher suffers from an 'overdose' of cannabis in his female pupil's bedroom only to realise that he can't take it. Or Irvine Welsh's first ever science-fiction story that takes place in Lothian, featuring alien space casuals who turn the universe upside down and leave you gasping for air. Alan Warner's protagonist wanders the streets of Edinburgh after a rave and buddies up with a bizarre crematorium attendant, who gets his kicks out of burning bodies. While in James Meek's 'Pop Life' a music junkie is reborn. The stories present a frantic range of grotesque and psychotic creatures who are mad and kicking. They swear, dance, vomit, fight and copulate, taking you for a raving heedless ride on the roller-coaster of pop life.

Children of Albion Rovers is a dynamic and exciting version of urban realism not to be missed by fans of alternative Scottish popular writing. Other might want to consider leaving their fingers off it!   *Eva Freischläger*

Colonies of the Mind

Robin Jenkins, *Leila*, Polygon £8.99; John Herdman, *Ghostwriting*, Polygon £7.99; David Deans, *The Peatman*, Polygon £8.99.

Colonial power-struggles in 1950's Malaysia; dark apocalyptic terrors in 1980's Edinburgh; existential reflections from the depths of a Highland peatbog, who knows when – three distinctive visions from three generations of writers testify to the continuing eclecticism and vitality of contemporary Scottish fiction. What links these novels, however, is just as fascinating as what appears to separate them.

Where to place Robin Jenkins' *Leila* within the most distinguished, and still most shockingly undervalued, fictional *ouevre* Scotland has produced this century poses something of an enigma. The novel's anatomy of native resistance to colonial control in a small Malaysian state marks a return to a startling group of Jenkins' novels from the 1950s and 60s which explored the analogous predicaments arising from the colonial encounter, of which *Dust on the Paw* (1961) – an study of inter-racial tension in Afghanistan – is the finest example. *Leila* addresses the same concerns of racism, hypocrisy and power, but with a formal economy and thematic sharpening of Scotland's complex relationship with the legacy of British imperial culture which reflect the disruptive subtleties of more recent novels like *Fergus Lamont* (1979) or *Willie Hogg* (1993).

As with all Jenkins, surface, setting and story are deceptively – disconcertingly – simple. In the oil-rich state of Savu, Andrew Sandilands, prim and calvinistic Vice-Principal of the Teacher Training College, is comfortable enough in his persona as colonial representative to play golf with the Sultan, the oligarch in collusion with the British presence but shrewd enough to permit token expression of the natives' increasing aspirations towards democratisation. Sandilands' infatuation with, and precipitate marriage to, the exotic and brilliant Leila, political activist and daughter of the Leader of the People's Party, plunges the couple into a vortex of conflicting

North Words

The Magazine from the North for Fiction and Poetry

Northwords is published three times yearly from the Highlands of Scotland. As well as work from Scotland, previous issues have had material from elsewhere in Britain, France, Finland, Japan, Canada etc. The aim of the magazine is to publish new writing of quality while reflecting the perspective from the Highlands.

Subscriptions
Special Offer until June 1997

Prices (inc. postage)	UK	Abroad
3 issues (plus any back issue)	£7.50	£10.50
6 issues (plus two back issues)	£12.00	£18.00
Back issues 1-11	£2.00 each	£3.00 each

NB Issue 3 is no longer available

Cheques or International Money Orders should be made payable to **Northwords** and sent to:
Northwords Subscriptions, West Park, Strathpeffer, Ross-Shire, Scotland IV14 9BT

and ever-shifting values where powerful tensions between innocence and disingenuousness, idealism and fanaticism, self-loathing and superiority create chronic dualities of moral perspective.

Ingeniously and effortlessly, narrative perspective consistently undermines the possibility of secure vantage-points of moral evaluation which the novel's dilemmas demand: even when Sandilands' consciousness dominates, it is weighed down with self-recrimination and self-justification. The choric presence of prejudiced expatriates has a satirical edge, but only until Sandilands finds that his love for Leila is tainted with traces of the same disease. Even the tempting equation which would exalt Leila as paragon in the fight to defend the powerless cannot hold: for Jenkins, it would seem that all forms of idealism or fanaticism involve degrees of ruthlessness which, in turn, make delusion of the self, and of others, inevitable.

Deceived deceivers, the tortured lovers become a metaphor for the political corruption which determines the global power-game in which they are caught: the novel's most moving moment comes when Sandilands watches, stricken with guilt and helplessness, the landing aircraft carrying the Scottish troops who have been sent to crush the peoples' quite legitimate protest, and to kill his wife. Sandilands' tortured awareness of his own complicity creates perhaps the most deeply riven closing ambiguity – the glimmer of a new love symbolising both compromise and courage – anywhere in Jenkins. *Leila* is based on actual events in Brunei in the 1950s which marked the dreadful climax of the 'Malayan Emergency', but in its profoundly challenging insights into the dreadful sophistication of the colonial aftermath and its implications for moral responsibility both individual and collective, it far surpasses its historical specificity.

While he is much too modest a writer to attempt to 'surpass' anyone, John Herdman's continuing fascination with dualism certainly justifies his publisher's claim that he represents 'a worthy successor to James Hogg and R L Stevenson'. As with Jenkins, duality in Herdman's work amounts to a great deal more than empty homage to literary precedent, or

the transparent spectre of the contemporary Scottish novelist wandering around aimlessly carrying the heads of celebrated *doppelgänger* – one under each arm – and bumping into clichés. *Ghostwriting*, while clearly indebted to the 19th century Scottish novel's obsession with division, also invites us to reinterpret that legacy afresh by confirming dualism as a dynamic creative instrument, endlessly amenable to variation. In this novel, Hogg's and Stevenson's manic private memoirists meet the postmodernist theorists they anticipated.

Leonard Balmain, third-rate creative writer going off the rails at fifty, is reduced to answering a newspaper advertisement for a ghost writer – 'a thoroughly postmodern thing to do'. He is hired by the sinister Torquil Tod to 'ghost' his autobiography and to attempt to 'justify' Tod's disturbing life, which centres around a world of contemporary paganism, dodgy faith healers and neurotic communes, and an obsessive *folie a deux* culminating in an unspeakable act of sacrifice. It is not part of Balmain's contract to establish the veracity of Tod's story, but as a biographer, he has no choice but to *narrate*, and all narration is interpretation. Inevitably, Balmain is narrating his own biography too, or the prelude to his own death, as his complicity with Tod's secrets means he is doomed to die at Tod's hands.

Cleverly, *Ghostwriting* manipulates a somewhat predictable story to investigate the paradoxes of narrative itself. The novel wears its intellectual sophistication lightly, gently raising a number of intriguing theoretical issues, not as arid abstractions, but seamlessly woven into the plot: the impossibility of attaining objective truth; the unverifiable nature of any biographical fact when imaginative identification comes into play; the dangers, indeed, of 'imagining' anything at all. As the appended narrative by Balmain's literary executor makes clear, language ultimately betrays us – quite literally, Balmain's word becomes his bond. The sequence of overlapping narratives, too – Balmain both inside and outside his subject, but always trapped in it – further complicate identities and multiply possible interpretations. Is Torquil Tod at some level simply a fictional projection, or alter ego, of Balmain's own psychotic condition, and the ghostwriting conceit an elaborate aggrandisement of his pathetic suicide into symbolic Death of the Author? Or is his loyal executor really his executioner? In the very act of writing, Herdman seems to suggest, we are haunted by others while we haunt ourselves.

If *Ghostwriting* enacts the deathly power of narrative, David Deans' alternately compelling and infuriating *The Peatman* inhabits the opposite extreme: writing degree zero, or the narrative of powerlessness. Here, the purpose of narrative is its purposelessness. The novel comprises the monologue of an anonymous narrator stuck in a bog amidst an expansive Highland landscape while stealing peats: the fusion of extreme isolation and stasis reveals a clear debt to the tactics of Beckett's trilogy. So, too, does the content of the narrative itself. 'I will omit the sad start', Dean's narrator begins. Except that the novel never begins, and never really ends. Compensating for the failures of a life which have left the anti-hero squatting alone in a sordid bothy and reduced to stealing fuel, he embarks upon reminiscences of a painful past which are repeatedly, chronically, halted and deferred by a compulsion to digress into realms of garrulous philosophical speculation. The material banality of the narrator's condition – ornate disquisitions on the intractable nature of broom handles, bin liners and dung heaps – is juxtaposed with glimpses of emotional intensity, all subjected to a highly elaborate discourse of quizzical metaphysical anxiety.

Thus the real subject of *The Peatman* becomes the endless referentiality of language itself, the domain in which the peatman is both wilfully and helplessly confined in his compulsion to narrate in any direction but towards the truths he cannot acknowledge. Such a summary might suggest that the novel is the literary equivalent of trying to set fire to sodden peat with a box of damp matches, but this would be to ignore the sardonic humour which illuminates the self-reflexive claustrophobia throughout. To paraphrase the novel's often hilarious parenthetical refrain, there's 'always some bastarding potential' for the narrator's addiction to language's multiple meanings to invest the (non-) proceedings with a scintillating wit. There's an anarchic and satirical dimension, too, in the novel's subversion of the icons of the culture, history and landscape of the Highlands, envisioned as an enmired and stultifying environment where everyone is called Mackenzie and it is only ever Sunday.

Love it or hate it, no recent fiction addressing life north of Dunkeld comes anywhere near the audacity and comic absurdity of Deans' demented revisions of the Highland Clearances as the story of the eradication of a fantastic species of flying sheep, to say nothing of the episode in which the peatman describes his taming of a seagull called Peter. There are pages of stylistic brilliance and great originality here, though one is left to doubt how the author's gifts might be developed in further directions in the aftermath of such an exhaustive (and often exhausting) *tour de force*. Is the author too bogged down by the weight of his endeavour? Possibly not. Even a novel as bizarre as this, with an anti-hero as unconventional, has recourse to the device of – surprise, surprise – the good old Scottish divided self, in the form of the peatman's alter-ego Jacques, who pops up from his box in the latter stages to parody the life of his hapless other half.

Always some bastarding duality.

Gavin Wallace

A Well-Plotted Novel

Moscow Stations, Venedikt Yerofeev, Faber and Faber, £14.99; *Floria Tosca*, Paola Capriolo, Serpent's Tail, £7.99; *The End of the Story*, Lydia Davis, Serpent's Tail, £8.99.

Aristotle tells us in his essay 'On the Art of Poetry', "Thus well-constructed plots must neither begin nor end in an haphazard way, but must conform to the pattern I have been describing," This means having a recognisable beginning, middle and end, in that order. In school we were taught that plots contained conflict, climax and resolution, but when we left we discovered that fiction, and the life it reflects, did not necessarily follow these prescribed patterns. Novels could start at the end or middle first or even more distressing to the reader have no uniform, mappable plot at all.

The three novels I will be discussing are from this school of writing. While their plot contortions force us to look at them carefully creating a deeper sense of mystery, the lack of a conforming plot and its reassuring conventions can leave the reader struggling to follow the author's twisting and slippery intentions.

Moscow Stations does have the structure of a plot, but it remains only a form on which the story is draped. Translated and adapted for the theatre by Stephen Mulrine of the Glasgow School of Art, it reached cult status in Russia before Yerofeev's tragic and self-predicted death in 1990. Set in Communist Russia the novel is based around a train journey from Moscow to Petushki where Yerofeev (the novel could be called semi-biographical) plans to visit his young son and his "golden-haired she-devil". Petushki, where the jasmine forever blooms, becomes a symbol of the fading opportunities left for Yerofeev and other contemporary Russian citizens.

Each section represents a certain length of the journey and as Yerofeev reaches the different stages he vacillates from clear-headed drunkenness to pure rambling. He becomes more delirious and desperate to reach Petushki. During the trip he speaks to angels and a Sphinx, gives recipes for cocktails such as 'Tears of a Komsomol Girl' and 'Dog's Giblets', discusses Russian literature and the effects of alcohol on its writers and tells about the time when he declared war on Norway.

Yerofeev, as an unreliable and unpredictable narrator, leads the reader astray from any hopes of a recognisable plot, a coherent story. One is left uncertain what is real or just a hallucination as Yerofeev almost has the reader seeing visions with him. Yet, his social commentary looks not just at his own time but also at modern Russia which has been unable to banish many of the ghosts Yerofeev writes about. His witty and frank view of human nature sees the beauty when it is often at its basest and most human. He never judges himself or his fellow travellers harshly.

Floria Tosca by Paola Capriolo also examines the inner thoughts of one man, allowing him to justify his actions to himself and the reader. The novel which is based on and parallels the action in the opera of the same name chronicles the slow turning of a mind from a self-righteous and misplaced crusade to insanity. Knowledge of the opera is helpful for following the story as the novel attempts to give further explanation to the main character's, the Baron Scarpia, terrible actions.

There is very little action in the novel for the reader to become caught up in as most of it takes place between the diary entries of the Baron Scarpia or in the opera itself. We are instead privy to the Baron justifying his unseen actions. At an early meeting with Tosca the Baron admits to torturing and killing prisoners in his role as chief of police, His justification is that "He (God) exhorts us to mortify the flesh" and the Baron has taken it upon himself to recognise the weaknesses of others and to hand out punishment. As Tosca continues to plead for exoneration for her lover, she and the Baron fall into a tighter circle of their own self-destructive natures.

The novel, though short, is ponderous to read. Though the Baron's reasonings are understandable given the entries of the diary following his madness, the same basis of understanding is not allowed the reader for Tosca's actions. The Baron is vain and despicable with his own sense of moral righteousness which makes the reader wholly unsympathetic to him or his fate. At the same time, Tosca herself remains a mystery.

Much the same could be said for the unnamed character in *The End of the Story.* The woman is not badly drawn by Lydia Davis, on the contrary she is totally believable. She is just unapproachable as a character and as a main player in the story.

The novel toys with the idea that the main character is writing the novel about her failed relationship. This act of creation is not told straight through, instead the woman jumps from episode to episode with no explanation why she picks that certain scene to expose. The character continually undermines herself by leaving out certain details or admitting she is uncertain to what really happened. She contradicts herself, changes her minds, tells the reader that she is deliberately leaving out something that would explain her actions.

What bothers me is that she didn't seem particularly in love with the man she was seeing or even seem to be missing him at the time of the novel's creation. She gives no reason why she was telling this particular story, why it affects her so much that she has to write about it years after the fact. She appears totally apathetic but driven by the novel. The woman's stalking of her ex-lover and her futile attempts to win him back seem completely unbelievable and by that late point in the novel any emotional tie with her that would help win the reader over is gone.

The novel appears to be the disinterested rambling story of a disinterested and unemotional character. That may have been the idea, though, to write a unstructured novel about an uneventful, unspectacular relationship. (Isn't that how most of them go anyway) The reason is never made clear why the reader should read the novel, as nothing happens.

Structure and plot are not necessary for an interesting and gripping novel, but something such as characterisation or mood must bring the reader into and keep them involved with the story when a strong storyline cannot. In the first two books I discussed the characters were strong and their psychology held the novels together when there was nothing going on but their own disorganized thoughts. Novels like these do not need the mundane constrictions of plot to interest the reader; the characters have a force of their own.

Gerry Stewart

■SCOTTISH■**BOOK**
COLLECTOR

Interview: James Hunter
Fillin' the Shelves: A
Residence at the Soutar
Hoose
by Robert Alan Jamieson
& Short Story by Iain Grant

Subscriptions (6 issues)
£10 (UK) £13.50 (EUR) $30 (US/Canada)
Free classified advert offer
to subscribers. More details from
SBC c/o 36 Lauriston Place
Edinburgh EH3 9EU
0131 228 4837
Please Note New Address

Pamphleteer

The small press has historically been one of the widest conduits for creative writing about women's issues. While the growing clout of the likes of Virago Press bodes well for the circulation of writing by, for and about women, it also has the potential to drain the small press of quality women's writing. The books covered here are concerned with women's role in modern society. They are only a few examples of the fine women's writing still coming out of small presses, which should not be overlooked.

Special Reserve (Scottish Cultural Press, PO Box 106, Aberdeen AB9 8ZE, £4.95) is a collection of writing by women who currently live in Aberdeen. It was compiled and published as part of the 1996 Aberdeen Women's Festival, with support from the Aberdeen District Council. Aside from living in Aberdeen, the authors have little in common. The result is a diverse collection, with a good representation of both poetry and prose. It encompasses settings from the UK to the Middle East, and topics from motherhood to child abuse.

Though the collection represents both unknown and well-known authors, the quality of the work is consistent. Among the best in the collection is Priscilla Frake. Her agile, accomplished use of language illuminates emotional aspects of what is often considered the mundane of domestic life. Much of the fiction included is outstanding, namely Leila Aboulela's sensitive portrayal of a child exploring the strictures of her culture in 'Tuesday Lunch,' and Anne Flann's 'O'Flaherty's Cat,' a humorous narrative utilising the familiar voice of the Irish storytelling tradition.

Special Reserve is not primarily a collection of Scottish writing or writing focusing on life in Aberdeen. Anyone looking for either will be disappointed. However, it works well as a collaboration of old-hands and newcomers from vastly different cultural backgrounds.

Broken Angels (Dionysia Press, 20A Montgomery Street, Edinburgh EH7 5JS, £4.50) is Susanna Roxman's first full-length collection of poems composed in English. The Swedish-born poet has Scottish roots, and has published previously in both languages. *Broken Angels* is primarily, though not exclusively, concerned with the woman's aging process, and her need to re-define herself in non-aesthetic terms. Roxman's past work in ballet and fashion modelling surface within her writing as does her near-fatal battle with anorexia.

The book is divided into eight parts, each loosely based on a separate subject. The tone, particularly of the first two sections, is cool, reserved and scholarly. This is detrimental to pieces with emotionally laden subject matter, such as 'The Peat Bog', which describes a bog-corpse excavation. Seamus Heaney's famous poems on the topic set a difficult precedent, and Roxman's broad, reticent observations fail to elaborate on it:

> He'd been ready for long when he went
> A bribe for this high-risk zone,
> he was hanged with a length of rope,
> then tipped into the sheer unknown.

However, with the third section, really a short poem cycle, Roxman hits her stride. She uses a Lapland trek for both structure and central metaphor. The language remains polished, but becomes far more personal. She takes more emotional risks, sounding the depths of her subject matter unexplored in the previous sections. The natural world becomes her vehicle for self-exploration, and as such, it pervades the imagery, as in 'Lapland':

> Here darkness means milk
> and all criteria prove invalid.
>
> I breathe on the moon till it mists
> but a rock throws its pointed
>
> head back and howls.

The underlying emotional trek is not an adroit progression: as on a physical trek there are unexpected emotional pitfalls. There are moments of splendour, as in 'Annual Rings':

> I stand wrapped in clear wood.
>
> My mind ripples endlessly, water
> thinking in all directions at once.
>
> I breathe with green and orange wings.

In the following sections, Roxman maintains this insight and sensitive understanding of her material, whether it is Pavlov's abandoned dogs or an ancient glass jar. *Broken Angels* is ultimately a rewarding collection, full of wisdom and perceptive observation.

When I Became an Amazon (Iron Press, 5 Marden Terrace, Cullercoats, North Shields, NE30 4PD, £5.99), a poem cycle written by Jenny Lewis and illustrated by Tinker Mather, is a small-press gem. A synergism of myth and modern story, it comprises suffering and optimism with an impact far beyond the 'women's issue' it technically examines.

Lewis' inspiration came from her own struggle with breast cancer, and the recently-discovered tombs of Iron Age warrior women – possibly the mythical Amazons – in Southern Russia. There are three narrators: an unnamed modern woman with breast cancer, an Iron Age Amazon girl called Oreithya, and the Amazons' Shaman, Oreithya's father.

Aided by Mather's primitivistic black-and-white illustrations, Lewis forges a linking metaphor using the modern reality of mastectomy, and the hypothesis that ancient woman warriors would have stunted the growth of one breast in order to wield a bow and arrow. The modern woman uses this idea as strength to face the loss of her own breast.

The book's ingenuity lies in the Iron Age sections, which are authentically free of feminist propaganda. Oreithya's monologues focus on her battle to rescue her mother, Hippolyta, from Theseus. The use of Hippolyta as an extraneous character anchors the fantasy in a familiar story, precluding lengthy explanations, and leaving more room to expand on the imagined world of the Amazons. Lewis' portrayal of this world is accomplished in the sections detailing Oreithya's travels:

> One evening we stopped by a lake which mirrored
> tops of mountains . . .
> . . . we stood at the edge of mysterious night,
> awed by the majesty and loneliness of those far spaces
> echoing with stars. The stillness called for us with tidal voices.

These sections read as translations. Their antiquated construction, combined with a reverence for nature and the tribe, create an authentic voice for an ancient woman.

The most thoroughly imagined sections are the Shaman's. He speaks in obliquely beautiful words of his love and respect for his wife and daughter, the pain of losing them continually to their campaigns, and the reverence he feels for his own role in the tribe:

. . . it was two
women who made me see how much love
I was capable of – my
lover

Hippolyta and our child, Oreithya. From
childhood I'd had the gift
of visions – been able to interpret signs,
stones falling at random;

The intertwined stories culminate in a strong message about the importance of accepting one's fate, and moving forward with that acceptance towards a hopeful future.

Though there is no dearth of literature on the situation in Northern Ireland, or the hard lot that often falls to its women, *Damaged Goods*, a play by Martin McCardie (dualchas, 1/R, 21 Garturk St, Glasgow) still manages some original thinking on both topics. At first glance, it is a static, predominantly cerebral piece: its bulk consists of a conversation between two boys in an abandoned Scout hut on the Liverpool docks. Michael O'Hanlon is Glasgow-born, but considers himself Irish, thanks to the anti-Brit brainwashing of his late Granda. Motivated by the desire to live up to his Granda's ideals, he holds Jeremy hostage in the hut. Michael intends to use the kidnapping to prove his worth to the IRA, who will then ostensibly allow him into their ranks.

The first half of the play contains some interesting twists of logic, and characterises the boys believably. Aside from two gratuitously long monologues, the dialogue is convincing and well-paced.

Static becomes kinetic with the introduction of the unnamed young woman in the second act. For most of this act, she is silent, giving Michael and Jeremy ample opportunity to display their own bigotry and sexism in their conversation about her:

> Jeremy: What about her, are you just going to leave her?
>
> Michael: Give me your laces. . . . They should do.
>
> Jeremy: What are you going to do?
>
> Michael: I'm going to tie her up with these.

The offensive position the woman ends up taking is surprising, and constitutes the true originality of the play. She manages to educate both Michael and her audience on a particularly gruesome facet of the struggles in Northern Ireland, in a manner which is uncomfortable, yet no more heavy-handed than the subject matter merits.

Cast in Clay/Cré na Cuimhne (Hu Publications, 49 Main Street, Greyabbey, Co. Down BT22 2NF) by Cathal Ó Searcaigh, translated by Frank Sewell, examines another aspect of women in Northern Ireland. The fifteen-page chapbook contains two poem cycles, 'Field of Bones' / 'Gort na gCnámh' and the title cycle, 'Cast in Clay.' The book reads one direction in English, and flips over to read the opposite direction in Irish Gaelic. This is a clever method of integrating the translation, though it leaves gaps at the beginning of each reading, which are a bit disconcerting.

'Field of Bones' is a harsh, first-person account of incest between a drunken father and his young daughter, resulting in unwanted pregnancy and infanticide. Though the topic is horrifying, the language is articulate and images powerful. 'Cast in Clay' is a very different kind of piece, again told in the first person, eulogizing an old man friend of the narrator. The writing here is still accomplished, but lacks the emotional vehemence of the first piece. For this reason, the pairing of the two is somewhat unbalanced – the violence of the first cycle overshadows the sentiment of the second. Both, however, are characterized by an intensity and articulation which signify clear talent. Like the rest, *Cast in Clay* is a small book full of big ideas, focusing on women's struggles but significant to everyone. All are well worth a read, and all exemplify the best of current small press publications.

As an aside, I'd like to mention another recent publication. For fifty years, the Edinburgh Writers' Club has offered support, guidance, and comradeship to Edinburgh-based writers, both unknown and well-established. To celebrate, the Club has published a Jubilee Anthology, including work by well over thirty writers, in prose and poetry, fiction and non-fiction, some with illustration. Obviously, the anthology encompasses a wide variety of subject matter and style, with contributions by both past and present members. It is worth owning a copy of this milestone collection.

Sarah Bryant

Catalogue

I approached both *Scottish Love Stories* (Susie Maguire, ed., Polygon, £9.99) and *Scottish Sea Stories* (Glen Murray, ed., Polygon, £9.99) with some trepidation. Books of short stories are often quite difficult to get into, and by their very titles, these works promised subject matters rather alien to my norm. The former hooked me quickest, through the introduction which sends up Barbara Cartland, Dynasty, Delia Smith and "wet midgey evenings". Anyone who follows up Dame Cartland with mention of someone who might "strap into leather and cruise when her day's work is done" and later asks if love is "worn beneath the kilt", gets my vote.

As Maguire says, there's "food for the soul of the cynic and the afflicted alike" with stories from Ian Hamilton Finlay, George Mackay Brown, Janice Galloway and Neil Gunn among others. Special mention must be made of Deirdre Chapman's 'The New Place', for the inclusion of the line "Her bosom spread itself splendidly beneath the surface [of the sea], her cleavage a cushioned grotto for tired plankton", and also for mentioning Rothesay in July!

Gordon Legge's 'I Never Thought it Would be You' has a 'girl power' theme, with the male narrator describing his other half as

a funny person, not a fun person, kind of privately witty as opposed to the more publicly wanton (i.e. thick) types [his mates] go for.

There are no pedestals – while sometimes "she was the trophy and [he] was the winner", just as often "she was the booby prize and [he] was the lumber." The stories vary in theme from broken engagements, through looking for love, enduring the little trials of love (meeting partners' mothers), to the love of 'untouchables' like Sean Connery. Most of them avoid slush to a large degree (sorry, Babs) and deal with love in a practical manner. And it works well. "Ooh, Baby, Yeah".

Scottish Sea Stories was more varied than I had expected. Eric Linklater's well-known 'Sealskin Trousers' appears and the presence of this tale, and 'The Kelpie of Corryvrechan', and 'The Mermaid and the Lord of Colonsay' suggests that not all the stories are going to be accounts of voyages done in a factual way; a fantasy element is allowed to creep in. There are tales from the likes of R L Stevenson and

Walter Scott, and George Mackay Brown appears again. There is also a Para Handy story by Neil Munro for those seeking some salty humour on the voyage. While enthusiasts are likely to know some of this collection already, it is a nice work to have at hand to dip into when the mood takes you.

One of the highlights of this *Catalogue* is *A Highland Lady in France* (ed. Patricia Pelly and Andrew Tod, Tuckwell Press, £9.99). *Memoirs of a Highland Lady* first introduced Elizabeth Grant of Rothiemurchus – the Canongate Classic edition was recently in the top five Scottish titles. The more recent work details Grant's life when she lived in France and is everything I look for in an autobiographical work. Essentially a diary, it includes a closely-observed commentary on life around the author, as opposed to being self-indulgently concerned with the writer herself. This reveals more about the woman's own character by her observations, and the personality that comes across here is probably far different to the one that she portrayed publicly as a lady of the 1840's.

Grant's biting comments on almost every topic, from social life to politics, are funny and unexpectedly intelligent – this challenges preconceived notions that ladies of her class only knew about 'women's matters'. She is often what would now be considered very politically incorrect, cheerfully stating after living for a while in France,

I am beginning to like the coloured handkerchief if the faces were only a little prettier, but there is no beauty, nor any grace . . . Individually they don't reward inspection.

Undoubtedly she is very superior, being unable to "understand the practical morality of [her] brother-in-law and [sister], both religiously disposed", who are in debt and borrowing money from all sources, yet still wildly extravagant. And often you can just see the glow of self-satisfaction:

Went to the shoemaker's, M. La Croix, a most agreeable-looking fat man with such beautiful eyes, told me I had a very pretty foot, was very clever and had the air of a person of consideration, shewing I had been well brought up, etc.

The Return of John Macnab (Headline Review, £16.99) by Andrew Greig opens with a letter by 'John Macnab' detailing his intention to "take a salmon or a brace of grouse or a deer, from the estates of Mavor, Inchallian and Balmoral respectively" as a challenge to those estates, with set terms and conditions. For further information, they are to consult *John Macnab* by John Buchan. The more observant will realise that the action is based in the Highlands, and there are nice touches like Greig's use of the intriguing sentence – "in the office of what we'll agree to call the *Deeside Courier*", making the reader wonder which local paper he's really thinking of.

The action revolves around 'John Macnab', but includes a variety of topics including sexual politics, land access and landownership disputes. For those fearing it sounds a bit detached from a more modern theme, worry not. One of the characters suns himself while "alternating between *The Acid House* and *Advanced Angling*", and Duncan McLean, one of the leaders of the new generation of Scottish writers, seems to love the book, calling it compelling and quirky, and, likening it to a cross between John Buchan and Iain Banks, advises the reader to "read and savour".

Reading and savouring is also appropriate with regard to *A Scottish Feast: an Anthology of Food and Eating*, by Whyte and Brown (Argyll Publishing, £9.99). Made up of extracts, the work includes such items as 'Miss Cranston's Tea Menu' and 'The River Bank' from Kenneth Grahame's *The Wind in the Willows*, and Sheena Blackhall's 'Aiberdonian Recipe', which, far from being about food, is a recipe for making an Aberdonian. There are also excerpts from Para Handy, and R L Stevenson's *Kidnapped*, as well as Scott's *The Antiquary*, so there's something to suit everyone's tastes.

There are a lot of offerings at the moment for history lovers. *John Knox House: Gateway to Edinburgh's Old Town* by Donald Smith (John Donald Publishers Ltd., £6.50) studies that medieval structure. As well as the history of the building itself, the lives of people connected to it are incorporated, including that of Sir James Mossman, goldsmith to Mary, Queen of Scots, and religious context is discussed. The book also answers frequently asked questions, such as "Did John Knox ever live in this house?" The answer? Well, if you're that interested . . .

For those more interested in the 'heroic'

territory of Scottish history, try John Barbour's *The Bruce* (Transl. by George Eyre-Todd, Mercat Classics, £11.99). Written in the 14th century, Barbour details the Bruce's story in the Wars of Independence and the battle of Bannockburn. Pervading the work is the importance of individual and national liberty. Definitely a must for enthusiasts.

The Scottish Record Office has a number of editions out in their *History at Source* series, detailing everyday life of Scots in history. Among the titles are: *The Crofters*; *The Peoples of Scotland: a Multi-cultural History*; *The Emigrants*; *The Scots in America*; *The Scots in Canada*; *The Scots in Australia* and *The Scots in New Zealand*. Included are historical backgrounds, lists of documents, extracts and facsimiles. Information is also given on how to use resources of the SRO.

Also well worth mentioning are some works of fairly varied themes. Thorbjörn Campbell's *Standing Witnesses* (Saltire Society, £16.99) documents stories of the Scottish Covenanters, and the whereabouts of their memorials – informative, it will be of value to any interested in the subject. Schoene's *The Making of Orcadia* (Peter Lang, £35.00) is a study of George Mackay Brown, and the effects of his background on his work, drawing on new concepts of narrative identity. *The Poems of Ossian* edited by Gaskill (EUP, £16.95) is an annotated edition of Macpherson's work, based on the 1765 text of the *Works of Ossian*, and includes all the Ossianic poetry, as well as criticism. Vivienne Couldrey's *Painters of Scotland* (Thomas and Lochar, £39.00) is an 'artistic tour' of Scotland and its painters of the last 200 years, and there are plenty of quality reproductions, as well as information on different areas and the artists themselves. For those who read Italian, *Scozia Controluce* by Valentina Poggi has been published by FaraEditore.

Lastly, Jim Crumley's *The Road and the Miles* is 'a homage to Dundee'. He begins by discussing the questionable 'Bonnie-ness' of Dundee, but, with the aid of Alfie, a fictional Dundonian, and the Dundee dialect, he manages to humorously intrigue and convince that perhaps Dundee is quite interesting and loveable after all.

CJ Lindsay

Notes on Contributors

Sarah Bryant lives in Massachusetts and has recently completed a M.Litt in Creative Writing at St. Andrews University.

Roger Caldwell: critic/reviewer on philosophy, music and literature. *This Being Eden*, forthcoming from Peterloo Press.

Maoilios Caimbeul: his home is in Staffin, Skye and he works as a Gaelic teacher in Gairloch High School. He has written a number of books in Gaelic.

Jon Corelis lives near San Francisco. His book of verse translations, *Roman Erotic Elegy*, was published in 1995 by the University of Salzburg Press.

Seán Damer is currently a self-employed writer, a part-time lecturer of Sociology at the University of Glasgow and a Tutor of Criminology with the Open University.

Bill Duncan was born in Fife and lives in Dundee. He has published poetry, prose and non-fiction in *Chapman, New Writing Scotland, Cencrastus* and *The Source*.

Angus Dunn writes short fiction and poetry, published in various anthologies and literary magazines. Lives in Ross-shire.

Trevor Edmands: painter, sculptor, writer? Lives in Sheffield. 'Short Fictions' have been published widely in U.S. including *Triquarterly* and *The Signal*.

Sally Evans' recent poetry books are *Looking for Scotland*, (University of Salzburg Press) and *Millennial*, (diehard).

Anne Frater has poems published in *Gairm* and *Chapman* and her first collection, Fo'nt t-Slige was published by *Gairm* in 1995.

Eva Freischläger: a Comparative Literature graduate currently teaching German in Glasgow and volunteering at Canongate.

Valerie Gillies' book, *The Ringing Rock*, is available from Scottish Cultural Press. She is writer in residence, University of Edinburgh.

Harry Gilonis is a part-Scots poet, editor, publisher and critic with an interest in marginal(ised) and peripheral(ised) writing.

Rody Gorman born Dublin 1960. Lives in Skye. His collection *Fax and Other Poems* was published by Polygon in 1996.

Neil K Henderson has been producing mainly humorous or fantastical work in a variety of forms, from 1987. His watchword is "Float like a butterfly – slink like an eel".

Elizabeth James's collection of short poems, *1 :50,000*, was published by Vennel Press in 1992. She works at the National Art Library,

Victoria and Albert Museum, London.

Robert Alan Jamieson is the author of three novels and a book of poems. Since 1993 he has been a co-editor of *Edinburgh Review*.

Eva Fleg Lambert: born in Germany, resident of Skye since 1971 where she breeds sheep for yarn and writes freelance.

C J Lindsay also known as Garfield is from Aboyne, Deeside. Writes and makes a living scaring people and being catty.

Maurice Lindsay: former programmer for Border Television. His many publications include *The Burns Encyclopaedia* and *The History of Scottish Literature*.

Patrick McEvoy, lecturer and writer, lives in Downpatrick, Co. Down. He has published poetry in several magazines and collections.

Colin Mackay is a night-watchman in Edinburgh and can't think of another buggering thing to say about himself.

Aonghas Macneacail is currently Writer in Residence at Sabhal Mor Ostaig in Skye. His latest collection is *An Oideachadh Ceart* (A Proper Schooling) from Polygon.

W S Milne: a disaffected lecturer, hairmless, sooth o the border, screivin in Scots for the enlichtenment of sinse.

Kevin MacNeil was born and raised on the Isle of Lewis. Has lived in Edinburgh and Skye. He has been widely published.

William Neill: poet and translator in Scots, Gaelic and English. *Selected Poems 1969-92* published by Canongate.

G A Pickin's stories have appeared in several anthologies. There may be more, if a mesmeric view of Ireland doesn't expand its disruptive influence.

Jonathan Tulloch has been published in *The European, Iron* and *Vigil*. He is currently looking for a publisher for his first novel, a development of the story published here.

Gael Turnbull's recent book of poems is *For Whose Delight* from Mariscat Press.

Gavin Wallace: lives in Fife. Co-editor of *Edinburgh Review* and Associate Lecturer with the Open University, he has written books on Scottish fiction and theatre.

Christopher Whyte is a novelist, poet and critic. His upcoming novel *The Warlock of Strathearn* will be published by Gollancz.

Jayne Wilding lives and writes poetry, poetic prose and short stories in Lochend, Edinburgh, finding inspiration from the wild places nearby.